Roman P

HOW TO LEAD
IN PRODUCT
MANAGEMENT

Practices to Align Stakeholders,
Guide Development Teams,
and Create Value Together

How to Lead in Product Management: Practices to Align Stakeholders,
Guide Development Teams, and Create Value Together
Roman Pichler
Copyright © 2020 Roman Pichler. All rights reserved.
Published by Pichler Consulting.
ISBN 978-1-9163030-0-3

Editors: Carolyn and Lara from Elite Authors
Layout: Booknook
Cover design: Ole H. Størksen
Cover photo: Shutterstock

CONTENTS

Preface..vii
  Who Should Read This Book.. viii
  Where the Ideas Come From.. viii
  A Brief Guide to This Book...ix

Introduction.. I
  Six Product Leadership Challenges...I
    No Transactional Power..2
    Large and Heterogeneous Group...2
    Limited Influence on Group Selection...3
    Dual Role..3
    Leadership at Multiple Levels...4
    Agile Processes..5
  Influence People and Encourage Change..5
    The Behavioural Change Stairway Model..6
    Empathy as a Key Leadership Quality..7
    Strengthening Your Capacity to Empathise...9
    Improve Your Expertise.. 10
    Secure the Right Management Support.. 11
  Choose the Right Leadership Style.. 12
    Be Attentive to People's Needs.. 13
    Consider the Situation You Are In... 14

Interactions... 16
  Build Trust... 16
  Partner with the Scrum Master.. 19
    What the Scrum Master Should Do... 19
    What the Scrum Master Should Not Do.. 20

Why You Shouldn't Take on Scrum Master Duties 21
Shoot Your Scrum Master Troubles 22
Guide the Development Team 23
Set the Team Up for Success 23
Give People a Choice 24
Let the Team Own the Solution 27
Don't Manage the Team 28
Effectively Interact with the Development Team 30
Give the Team Time to Experiment and Learn 34
Lead the Stakeholders 36
Involve the Right People 36
Build a Stakeholder Community 38
Involve the Individuals in Product Discovery and Strategy Work 42
Engage the Key Stakeholders in Product Development Work 43
Don't Tolerate Inappropriate Behaviour 44

Goals 46
A Chain of Goals 46
Product Vision 48
User and Business Goals 49
Product Goals 50
Sprint Goal 51
Make Your Goals Great 51
Be Goal-Led, Not Goal-Driven 53
Set Realistic Goals 54
Choose Ethical Goals 56
Give People Ownership 58

Conversations 60
Listen Deeply 60
Why Listening Really Matters for Product People 61
Covey's Listening Levels 62
Listen Inwardly 64
Give the Other Person Your Full Attention 65
Listen with an Open Mind 67
Listen for Facts, Feelings, and Needs 68
Listen with Patience 71
Speak Effectively 72
Well Intended 72

True 74

Beneficial 75

Kind 79

Well Timed 82

A Summary of Selected Conversation Techniques 83

Conflict **85**

Avoid These Common Pitfalls 86

Win-Lose 86

Truth Assumption 89

Problem-Solving Mode 91

Blame Game 92

Artificial Harmony 93

Resolve Conflict with Non-Violent Communication 95

Overview of the Framework 96

Before You Start 98

Share Observations 101

Explore Feelings 102

Uncover Needs 105

Make and Receive a Request 106

When You Can't Resolve the Conflict 108

Decision-Making and Negotiation **110**

The Benefits of Collaborative Decision-Making 110

Set Yourself Up for Success 113

Engage the Right People in the Right Way 113

Employ a Dedicated Facilitator 115

Foster a Collaborative Mindset 116

Set Ground Rules 117

Choose a Decision Rule 118

Unanimity 119

Consent 121

Majority and Supermajority 121

Product Person Decides after Discussion 122

Product Person Decides without Discussion 124

Delegation 125

Take the Right Decision-Making Steps 126

Step 1: Gather Diverse Perspectives 127

Step 2: Build Shared Understanding 128

Step 3: Develop an Inclusive Solution 129

Tips for Negotiating Successfully 131
    Cultivate a Friendly Attitude..132
    Listen Deeply...133
    Don't Bargain over Positions..134
    Develop Options Together 136
    Reach Closure...137
Make Negotiation the Exception, Not the Norm 138

Self-Leadership 140
  Practise Mindfulness 140
    Mindfulness in a Nutshell 141
    Benefits of Developing Mindfulness 143
    Hold Personal Retrospectives..144
    Write a Journal...145
    Meditate...146
  Embrace a Growth Mindset 148
    What Is a Growth Mindset?..148
    Leverage Failure..149
    Foster an Open Mind 150
    Learn Something New 151
  Cultivate Self-Compassion..152
  Carefully Manage Your Time...153
    Adopt a Sustainable Pace 153
    Do One Thing at a Time...155
    Don't Neglect the Important but Less Urgent Work............155
    Take Regular Breaks 158

Acknowledgements...159

About the Author...160

References...161

Index 165

PREFACE

No matter how it looks at first, it's always a people problem.
Gerald Weinberg

Being a successful product manager or product owner does not only require the right hard skills—for example, the ability to interview users, create an effective product strategy and actionable product roadmap, prioritise and manage the product backlog, and apply the right metrics. While these skills are undoubtedly important, they are not enough. Products are developed, provided, and enhanced by people, and being able to effectively lead them is crucial to achieve product success. In other words, you can possess an extensive knowledge about advanced product management techniques, deep insights into the market your product addresses, its technologies, and the competition, but if you lack the right leadership skills, you will struggle to succeed in your job. This book helps you improve your capability to lead others and yourself. It helps you reflect on your current leadership ideas and behaviours and offers a collection of practical techniques to align stakeholders, guide development teams, and create value together.

Who Should Read This Book

I wrote this book with people in mind who work as product managers or Scrum product owners—who are responsible for making or keeping a product successful and for maximising the value it creates. I refer to these individuals as *product people* and *product person*, respectively, in order to avoid any negative connotations the reader might associate with the terms *product manager* and *product owner*.[1] But you will also benefit from reading this book if you manage a team of product people or a product portfolio or product part like a feature or component. The main practices covered, which include goal setting, listening and speaking, conflict resolution, and decision-making, are applicable whenever you lead and collaborate with others.

To get the most out of this book, you should be familiar with core product management concepts and techniques. If you lack this knowledge, you might struggle with some of the examples used. The book assumes that you work with or are familiar with agile practices and that your development team uses a framework like Scrum or Kanban, or at least some of their elements.

Where the Ideas Come From

Before I wrote this book, I researched as much of the leadership literature as I possibly could. My hope was to find a leadership model and adapt it for product management. But the more research I did, the more it became clear to me that none of the frameworks I found was a perfect fit: No model took into account the specific challenges that product people face, including having no transactional power and playing a dual role that involves leadership and active contribution. Instead of subscribing to a specific leadership model, I have carefully selected and combined practices from different frameworks

---

1   Thanks to Rich Mironov for introducing the term to me.

that I have found valuable in my work over the last fifteen years, both being a product person in my own business leading a dispersed team and teaching and coaching other product people, as well as advising companies to develop their product people into empowered, inspirational leaders. Additionally, I have applied Buddhist insights, due to my background as a practicing Buddhist. These include mindfulness, open-mindedness, and compassion. I believe that at its heart, leadership is about supporting and guiding people; it means caring about others as well as looking after yourself. I have made every effort, though, to avoid any form of dogmatism, and I truly hope that you will find this book helpful, no matter what your preferred leadership theory and spiritual practice may be.

A Brief Guide to This Book

I've written this book so that you can read its chapters individually, without necessarily having to read it front to back. At the same time, I have ordered the chapters so that they build on one another in a meaningful way. However you prefer to read the book, I recommend that you start with the chapters *Introduction* and *Interactions*. The former lays the basis for the remainder of the book, including the key leadership challenges product people face as well as techniques for influencing others and helping them change for the better. The latter discusses roles and responsibilities as well as building trust and establishing rapport with stakeholders and development teams. Note that this book covers a lot of ground. Like my other books, it is intended to provide a solid overview of the subject matter and to discuss helpful practices. It encourages you to reflect on your leadership behaviour, try out new practices, and become a better product leader.

INTRODUCTION

True leaders understand that leadership is not about them but about those they serve.
It is not about exalting themselves but about lifting others up.
Sheri L. Dew

This chapter covers important aspects and success factors in order to align stakeholders and guide development teams. It helps you reflect on the challenges you are likely to face, strengthen your authority and ability to influence others, and embrace the right leadership style, thereby forming the basis for the remainder of this book.

Six Product Leadership Challenges

While helping a group of people achieve shared goals is a general leadership objective, I find that there are six common challenges that make leading stakeholders and development teams special: As the person in charge of the product, you typically lack transactional power; you lead a comparatively large and heterogeneous group; you have limited influence on the group member selection; you actively contribute to reaching the goals while guiding others; you offer strategic and tactical leadership; and you usually work with agile practices, as I discuss at the end of this section.

Who Are the Stakeholders and Development Team Members?

A *stakeholder* is anybody with an interest in your product. In this book, I use the term to refer to those employees whose help you need to provide the product—for example, a sales rep who creates the sales strategy, a marketer who markets the product, or someone from legal or finance whose expertise is required.

A *development team* is a group of people who jointly develop a product or product part, like a feature or component.[2] The group has usually no more than ten members, and the individuals have all the skills required to design, implement, test, and document the product. Consequently, a development team may consist of user-experience designers, software architects, programmers, and testers. Additionally, it can be helpful when dev teams are stable, collocated, and autonomous. The former two qualities facilitate effective teamwork; the latter helps teams quickly innovate.

No Transactional Power

Unlike a line manager, you are not the boss; you don't manage the development team and stakeholders, and the individuals usually don't report to you. You consequently don't have any transactional power: You cannot tell the group members what to do; you cannot assign tasks to them; and you are typically not in a position to offer a bonus, pay raise, or other incentives. At the same time, you rely on their work. For example, the individuals may design, implement, market, sell, and support the product. Additionally, some of the people you lead might be more senior than you. They might have worked longer for the company, and they might be very influential and well connected.

Large and Heterogeneous Group

The group you lead can be large and heterogeneous. The development team is typically cross-functional: The members have different backgrounds and skills, including design, software development, and testing. Add the stakeholders to the mix who come from different

---

2   I use *feature* to refer to a product part that users can interact with, like search and navigation on an online retailer's website, and *component* to describe an architecture building block, such as a service, component, or layer.

business units—for example, marketing, sales, support, and service for a commercial product—and you will end up with a very diverse group that can easily comprise fifteen people.[3] Understanding the group members' different perspectives and needs and effectively guiding everyone can therefore be challenging.

Limited Influence on Group Selection

While you should try to get the right people on board, as I explain in the chapter *Interactions*, you can't always choose who the team members and stakeholders are, and you are typically not in a position to hand-pick people. Instead, you often rely on line management to staff the development team and to select representatives from the business units as stakeholders—no matter how likeable you find the individuals and how well you get on with them. Likewise, you usually don't have control over how long people will work with you: While it's beneficial to form a stable group whose members work with you on a continued basis, people might leave or join the group based on shifting business needs.

Dual Role

While guiding people can be challenging on its own, you also have to actively contribute to reaching the shared goals and achieving product success. In this sense, you play a dual role: You are leader and contributor. The former involves ensuring that the various workstreams, such as designing and building the product, preparing its release, and supporting it, are aligned—for instance, by encouraging key stakeholders to participate in sprint review meetings. It also comprises regularly assessing product performance and monitoring progress against the product roadmap. Additionally, you may have to coach or mentor

---

3   This number assumes that the development team has up to ten members. Compare the number with line managers, who typically look after seven to ten people in my experience.

some of the individuals and help them acquire the relevant product knowledge so that they can do a great job. As if this were not enough, you also have to help progress the product—for instance, by observing and interviewing users, analysing user feedback and data, revising the product strategy, adapting the product roadmap, prioritising the product backlog, and creating new user stories.

Leadership at Multiple Levels

Guiding the development team and stakeholders towards product success requires leadership at three levels: vision, strategy, and tactics. As the person in charge of the product, you should shape the vision of your product; you should lead the effort to create, validate, and evolve an effective strategy; you should guide the development of a product roadmap; and you should work with the development team on the product backlog to determine, capture, refine, and prioritise its items. This ensures that leadership and decision-making are consistent: The vision should guide the strategy, and the strategy should direct the tactics. At the same time, insights gained on the tactical level—for example, by testing prototypes or product increment with users—should inform the strategy, which in turn might impact the vision.

Shared Product Leadership

Products can grow too big for one person to provide guidance at all three levels. A common way to share product ownership is to have one person in charge of the overall product and individuals owning product parts, like features and components. You may therefore end up with an overall product owner or manager who closely works with feature and component owners.

Another approach, made popular by the scaling framework SAFe, is to split strategic and tactical responsibilities. This results in employing a person making strategic product decisions and one or more individuals looking after the tactical work and managing the product backlog. This option, however, is only recommendable in my experience for mature, stable products whose strategy is unlikely to change significantly.[4]

---

4   See Pichler (2016, "Scaling the Product Owner Role") for more information on how several product people can share product leadership and effectively collaborate.

Agile Processes

Most digital products are developed using an agile development framework like Scrum or Kanban. An agile process puts requirements on your interaction with the development team and, to a certain extent, the stakeholders. For example, an agile team is self-organising. This includes the right to determine the appropriate workload, reject work items if they exceed the team's capacity, and only work on what has been agreed for a sprint or what is within the agreed work in progress (WIP) limits.[5] These rules increase productivity and create a healthy, sustainable work environment. But they mean that you can't push work on to the team or interfere with the work during a sprint. Instead, the development team pulls work from the product backlog. Additionally, you have to make yourself available to the dev team, jointly work on the product backlog, participate in meetings like sprint planning and review, answer questions, and provide feedback on *done* pieces of work.[6]

Influence People and Encourage Change

Leading people comprises influencing and supporting the individuals to jointly work towards shared goals—for example, acquiring new users, retaining existing customers, or increasing revenue. But as the person in charge of the product, you usually don't have the authority to tell people what to do, as mentioned before. How can you then influence people and encourage individuals to be, for instance, more open to the ideas of others and more willing to co-operate with them?

---

5   WIP stands for "work in progress." A WIP limit prevents bottlenecks in software development and ensures a smooth flow of work. If the WIP limit has been reached, people can't take on more work.

6   A work item is typically "done" if it is implemented, tested, documented, and ready to be deployed.

The Behavioural Change Stairway Model

A not dissimilar but more extreme challenge was encountered by the FBI, the Federal Bureau of Investigation in the United States. Imagine that you are faced with the following situation: Armed terrorists have kidnapped a group of civilians. They are now asking for a ransom, and they are threatening to kill the hostages if their demands are not fulfilled. If you grew up with 1980s Hollywood movies like I did, you might be tempted to suggest sending in a Rambo-like agent who singlehandedly frees the hostages and captures the terrorists. In the real world, however, this approach has a low success and high death rate. The FBI therefore developed a different method, called the *behavioural change stairway model* (Voss 2016), which is based on the following insight: In order to encourage change in another person, you have to be able to influence the individual. To do so, you first need to establish a trustful relationship with the person. This is only possible if you empathise with the individual, understand her or his perspective, and take a genuine interest in the person's needs. And the best way to understand someone is to actively listen to the person, as figure 1 shows.

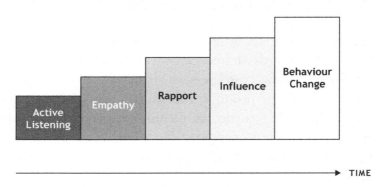

Figure 1: *Behavioural Change Stairway Model*

Figure 1 suggests that the best way to influence someone and encourage the person to change is to carefully listen to the individual, empathise with the person, and build a trustful relationship. You cannot skip any of the steps. Instead, you have to be patient and take one step at a time.

While I do hope that your challenges in guiding stakeholders and development teams are not quite as bad as the FBI's, my experience suggests that the behavioural change stairway model is directly applicable to product management. Here is why: People will only follow you for two reasons—because they trust and respect you or because they fear you. Coercing people to do something is undesirable: It never results in motivated individuals who are committed to achieving shared goals. Instead, it creates an unhealthy work environment where people act out of fear and obligation, and it destroys creativity, informed risk-taking, and innovation. Additionally, this option is usually not available to product people—you normally don't have the authority to tell people what to do, as I've mentioned before. If you want people to truly trust and respect you, then you have to show them that you genuinely care for them and that you are interested in their perspectives and would like to understand their needs. In other words, you have to strengthen your ability to empathise with others.

Empathy as a Key Leadership Quality

Empathy is our capacity to understand other people's feelings, needs, and interests and to take the perspective of the other person. Empathy entails a warm-hearted, open, and kind attitude. Being empathic means to care about and accept the other person—no matter if we agree with her or his views or if we like or dislike the person. As the behavioural change stairway model shows, we can empathise with people whose actions we deeply disagree with and who we might dislike. An FBI agent will most likely disagree with the terrorist she or he negotiates with, and the individual probably won't find the hostage taker a very likeable person. But this doesn't prevent the agent from empathising with the terrorist, taking a genuine, warm-hearted interest in the individual, and treating the person as a fellow human being, despite her or his deplorable actions.

The same is true for you: No matter how difficult or challenging a stakeholder or development team member might be, the best way to help them change is to empathise with them. If you tell people what they should need without carefully listening to them and taking a respectful interest in their underlying needs, the individuals are unlikely to follow your advice, even if you are factually right. In order to take on your advice, people first need to feel heard and understood.

Empathy is possibly the most important leadership quality: It not only allows you to influence others and encourage change but also creates trust and psychological safety—an environment in which people feel safe to speak up and are comfortable to be themselves. By cultivating empathy, you also increase the chances to understand the needs of your users and customers. "Empathy...moves us beyond thinking of people as laboratory rats or standard deviations," as Brown (2009, 49) puts it.[7] What's more, cultivating empathy will make you a more likeable and happier person: Connecting with others enriches our experience as human beings. Bear in mind, though, that your interest in the other person must be genuine. If you pretend to care or if you empathise only to get someone to do something, then people will sooner or later recognise your intention and stop trusting you.

All Smiles?

Being empathic does not require you to be happy and smiley all the time, nor does it mean sugar-coating messages, only telling people what they want to hear, and ignoring issues. Instead, it means caring about the other person and wanting to help the individual as much as is possible. This may well mean confronting someone's behaviour. For example, imagine that a stakeholder regularly fails to attend product strategy workshops and requests product roadmap changes by talking to you one to one. You should then consider asking the individual to change her or his behaviour, stop requesting roadmap changes, and attend the strategy sessions. But act in an empathic way: Find out what's going on with the individual and try to

---

7   Developing empathy is the first step in design thinking, an innovation process originally created by IDEO.

understand why she or he has not attended the workshops before you share your request. At the same time, be frank. Don't beat around the bush, but make a clear and specific request.[8]

Strengthening Your Capacity to Empathise

We all have the capacity to empathise. But sometimes it is difficult to take perspective and to comprehend what's going on for the other person. There are two common barriers to empathy: First, we can be so caught up in our own thoughts and stories that our ability to be receptive to the needs of others is reduced. The same is true when we are tense, irritated, or worried: Experiencing negative mental states makes it harder to relate to and understand others.

Second, we might confuse projection with empathy: The former means making assumptions about what the individual should feel according to preconceived ideas—for example, believing that someone who speaks loudly wants to dominate and take over the meeting. Empathy, however, implies developing an understanding of what is really going on for the other person. In the example mentioned, the individual might just have an odd communication habit and a general tendency to speak loudly, or the person might raise her or his voice because the individual is upset or wants to hide her or his worries.

Servant Leadership

Robert Greenleaf, who coined the term *servant leadership,* suggests that effective leadership starts with the desire to serve and help others, not to gain a personal benefit (Greenleaf 2002, 27). He also proposes that leaders should care about their followers, be concerned about their well-being, and ensure that their highest-priority needs are being served. This is in stark contrast to a view that regards people as resources, as a means to maximise personal and business benefits.

While you might disagree with Greenleaf's views or dislike the term *servant leader,* becoming aware of your true intention to lead others is important. It not only helps you decide if you should take on a leadership role but also helps you to effectively play the role and lead others. To put it differently, being an effective leader requires

---

8   I discuss speaking practices that help you convey difficult messages in more detail in the chapter *Conversations.*

> you to cultivate a genuine caring attitude for the people you want to lead, whether you like them or not. If this intention is not present in you, then you may not be ready yet to lead others.

In order to overcome these barriers and strengthen your capacity to empathise, work on your ability to be mindful of your mental state and lead with presence, as I discuss in more detail in the chapter *Self-Leadership*. Additionally, come from a place of curiosity and care: Take a genuine interest in the other person, make an effort to listen with the intention to understand, and refrain from prematurely judging what the individual is saying. Imagine being in the position of the other person. What would this be like?[9]

Improve Your Expertise

In addition to strengthening your capacity to empathise with others, make sure you have the necessary expertise. If your understanding of, for example, user and customer needs is insufficient, or if you are not aware of market trends and the competition, it will be hard for people to trust and follow you. Becoming a competent, well-rounded product person requires a continued learning effort in my experience. There are two reasons for this: First, product management is a multifaceted and comparatively young profession that is still changing.[10] Second, there is no standard education path, at the time of writing, to become a product professional. As product people, we therefore have the challenge not only to acquire a wide range of skills but also of different education backgrounds. Some of us may have started our careers in marketing, others in development, sales, or project management, for instance.

---

9   I've borrowed the expressions *lead with presence* and *come from a place of curiosity and care* from Sofer (2018).

10   To my knowledge, dedicated product management groups started to become more common from the 1950s onwards, and digital or software product management was introduced in the 1980s.

I would therefore encourage you to systematically develop your product management skills. Regularly reflect on your knowledge and skill set and identify gaps and shortcomings. Consider your leadership, strategic, and tactical skills.[11] Then choose the ones that need to be addressed and determine the right learning and development measures, be it by reading books and articles, watching videos, attending a public training course, or hiring a product mentor or coach. Embracing a growth mindset, as I describe in the chapter *Self-Leadership*, will help you sustain your learning journey.

Secure the Right Management Support

Last but not least, your ability to influence and lead others is affected by the management support you receive. If you don't have a management sponsor who can act as an adviser and escalation partner, then it may be harder for you to be respected by the stakeholders and development team. As a rule of thumb, the more important your product is, the more senior the sponsor should be. Additionally, if the product management maturity is low in your company—if, for example, there is no dedicated product management group or well-defined product roles—then people may not understand why you should be authorised to make product decisions, and it will be harder for you to guide and align others. In order to find the right management sponsor or help your company improve its product management maturity, partner with the Scrum Master, as I discuss in more detail in the chapter *Interactions*. But be aware that organisational change can be slow: Establishing an effective product management group may take many months or even several years.

---

11 See Pichler (2017) for more information on identifying gaps and shortcomings in your product management skill set.

Choose the Right Leadership Style

Most of us have ideas about what good leadership is and how great leaders act. For example, at an early stage of my career, I was invited to an assessment centre, where my leadership potential was evaluated. While the feedback I received was positive, the assessors told me that in order to succeed as a leader, I should be more directive. This surprised me for two reasons: First, people who know me well usually don't think that I lack assertiveness. Second, I've never agreed with the view that a strong leader is someone who acts in a dominant or authoritarian way. But as this story shows, different people and organisations have different ideas of what effective leadership entails.

Over the past decades, researchers have identified various leadership styles to describe common leadership behaviours.[12] For example, a *visionary* leader is someone who aligns people through a shared inspirational goal, a *democratic* or *participatory* leader is inclusive and involves people in decisions, an *affiliative* leader connects people and builds teams, a *delegative* leader empowers others to make decisions, a *coaching* leader develops people by helping them reach their goals, a *pacesetting* or *directive* leader sets standards and shows people how to move forward, and an *autocratic* leader makes the decisions and tells people what to do.

Distinguishing different styles can help you become aware of your preferred leadership behaviours. For instance, you might lean towards being an affiliative and delegative leader, as you like to care for the individuals, encourage teamwork, and let people work out for themselves what needs to be done. Or your preference might be a directive style, where you set standards and ask people to follow them. To better understand what your default leadership behaviour is, bring to mind a difficult situation you recently experienced and honestly reflect on how you communicated and acted. What did you say? And how did

---

12   See, for instance, Goleman, Boyatzis, and McKee (2013). The authors distinguish six leadership styles: visionary, coaching, affiliative, democratic, pacesetting, and commanding. Thanks to Geoff Watts for introducing them to me.

you say it? Did you resort to being authoritarian and tell people what to do? Or did you possibly gravitate towards the other extreme and watch people sort things out?

When carrying out this exercise, be careful that your ideas about how you *should* behave don't interfere with your analysis. Additionally, don't be self-judgemental and don't beat yourself up: We all have leadership preferences that are based on past experiences, the organisation we work in, and our beliefs and ideas; none of us is a perfect leader. What's more, there simply is *no one right way to lead people*. If you lean towards a visionary style, then this is helpful, for instance, when kicking off the development effort for a new product or a major product update. But the same behaviour probably won't be appropriate when stakeholders fail to meet a product roadmap goal or the development team repeatedly misses the sprint goal. You should therefore be flexible in your leadership approach and balance the different leadership styles depending on the needs of the stakeholders and the situation you find yourself in.[13]

Be Attentive to People's Needs

In order to be an effective leader, attend to the needs of the development team and stakeholders and take into account *group cohesion* and *expertise*. Newly formed groups with members hardly knowing each other typically require more support and often benefit from a more hands-on, directive leadership approach. For example, if you told a new development team to decide for themselves how to contribute to the product backlog work, they may well look at you with surprise and confusion. Instead, it might be more helpful to show people how to create effective user stories. Similarly, groups with little knowledge about the market, product, process, and relevant tools require more support. For example, if you ask the stakeholders how they want to

---

13   The discussion in the following two paragraphs is loosely based on Sosik and Jung (2011, 48), who suggest that effective leadership is centred on three components: leader, followers, and situation.

capture the product roadmap, then they may well feel overwhelmed if the individuals have never worked with such a plan. It might be better to suggest a specific roadmap format and jointly develop the plan.

But as a group gels and becomes more cohesive, and as people acquire the relevant expertise, you should adapt your leadership approach. You might be able, for instance, to delegate some of the user story refinement work to the development team, as suggested earlier, or you might want to explore with the stakeholders whether a different product roadmapping format or tool would be more helpful. And when stakeholders and dev team members change, group cohesion and expertise are likely to change too. Consequently, you may have to adapt your leadership style again.

If you are not quite sure what guidance people need, then ask them. Retrospectives are a great opportunity to collect feedback from the development team and stakeholders, understand if you effectively guided them, and adapt your leadership behaviour as appropriate. After all, leadership is not only about achieving results and getting things done. It's equally important to pay attention to how we accomplish the desired outcomes: What is the impact of your leadership style on the stakeholders and development team members? And what effect does it have on you? Does it support a healthy and creative work environment, or does it cause people to feel stressed or intimidated?

Consider the Situation You Are In

Finally, take into account the situation you are in. This includes your company with its unique culture, the overall business context, and the performance of groups and individuals. For example, in a company that has only recently started to value teamwork and is still characterised by strong hierarchies and a command-and-control management approach, you may find that people need plenty of encouragement to share ideas and to take on full responsibility for their work. It may therefore take a while before the stakeholders and team members start to appreciate an inclusive and delegative leadership style.

Similarly, if the business is struggling or even in crisis mode, you may find that people are worried and more concerned about their jobs than the success of the product and team. Consequently, a visionary and affiliative style might not be beneficial at this point in time, but the individuals may require a more directive approach. Finally, if you find that individual stakeholders or the development team struggle to meet agreed goals, then you should not turn a blind eye to this issue but address it. If the dev team, for example, has repeatedly not met the sprint goal despite you having analysed the issue in a sprint retrospective and agreed on actionable improvements, then do address the issue. Listen to and empathise with the individuals; don't blame people, and don't use harsh speech. But make it clear that the team is accountable for achieving an agreed sprint goal and that recurrently failing to meet the goal is not acceptable. This may require you to be assertive and possibly directive, even if you much prefer an affiliative or delegative style.

INTERACTIONS

The strength and endurance of a company does not come from products or services but from how well their people pull together.
Simon Sinek

Establishing the right interactions with the people you lead is crucial to provide effective leadership. This chapter discusses the roles and responsibilities of the Scrum Master, development team, and stakeholders; offers practices for interacting with the individuals at the right time and in the right way; and explains the focus and boundaries of your leadership.

Build Trust

Trust is the magic ingredient that allows relationships to blossom. To trust someone means to have faith in the person, to believe that her or his intentions are good and that acting on the individual's advice will be beneficial. When you trust a person, you feel safe in her or his presence and you are comfortable to speak your mind.

Trust is crucial for two reasons: First, when people don't trust each other, their interactions tend to be superficial. They often avoid making tough decisions that involve disagreements and conflict, and they are unable to effectively collaborate (Lencioni 2002, 91). That's bad news for your product: Successful products are not built on weak compromises or the smallest common denominator but on the collective expertise of the development team and stakeholders. What's more, without effective collaboration, it will be hard for you to achieve product success: You need the help of others to design, develop, and provide the product. Second, when people don't trust you, they won't wholeheartedly follow your lead but will act out of obligation at best. Gaining people's trust is therefore vital to guide and align people and to move forward together.

The following tips will help you build trust with the development team members, the stakeholders, the Scrum Master, and—if you develop a bespoke product—the client:

- *Come from a place of curiosity and care.* Reach out to people with warm-heartedness, take a genuine but respectful interest in the individual, and be concerned for her or his well-being.[14]
- *Listen with an open mind.* Make an effort to attentively listen, and don't prematurely judge or reject an individual's idea or concern. Be grateful for someone's contribution, even if you disagree. This makes people feel valued, and it encourages them to be open and trustful with you.[15]
- *Speak and act with integrity.* Say what is true; don't bend the truth or tell half-truths. Make your actions match your words; walk your talk. Avoid harsh and divisive words when criticising an idea or opinion. Always treat the other person with respect. Be willing to show vulnerability and admit mistakes: Don't pretend, boast, or talk badly about others.
- *Get to know people and allow people to get to know you.* We are all influenced by our backgrounds, family situations, and interests. Sharing this information is useful for two reasons: First, it helps

---

14 See the chapter *Introduction* for more information on cultivating empathy. I have borrowed the term *come from a place of curiosity and care* from Sofer (2018).
15 I discuss listening practices in more detail in the chapter *Conversations*.

people understand each other. It makes it clearer why somebody thinks and acts in a certain way. Second, sharing personal information is a trust-building exercise, as it requires people to open up. It can be particularly helpful to share failure stories, as Lencioni (2002, 64) recommends. This shows vulnerability, which in turn creates trust. If you use this exercise, then take the lead by sharing one of your failures. Even seemingly small activities, like having lunch or coffee together, can be helpful in getting to know the individuals.

- *Involve people in product decisions* and encourage them to share their ideas and concerns. Carefully listen to everyone, appreciate people's input, and respect their perspectives. This will increase people's trust in you.[16]

- *Be supportive and offer help* whenever possible and appropriate. This shows that you care for others and have good intentions. Make sure, though, that you help people to become self-sufficient. Avoid telling them how to do their jobs and instead offer guidance and direction.

- *Strengthen your product management expertise.* The more relevant knowledge you have about the market, users, and your product, and the more you are able to effectively apply product management practices—like creating a product strategy, developing a product roadmap, and validating ideas—the more likely it is that people will trust and follow you.

How Can I Tell That People Trust Each Other?

When people trust each other, they are open and honest with one another. The individuals don't shy away from addressing difficult issues and engage in constructive debates. At the same time, people tend to be friendly towards each other and are comfortable in one another's company.

If, however, a group of people lacks trust, the mood is often subdued. There is little debate, and people are careful not to say something that is perceived as wrong. Everyone typically wants to be involved in every decision, and often there is an artificial harmony that hides underlying issues and disagreements.

---

16 I talk more about involving the dev team and stakeholders in product decisions in the chapter *Decision-Making and Negotiation.*

Partner with the Scrum Master

While establishing an effective relationship with the development team and stakeholders is undoubtedly important, I find that product people often underestimate the significance of effectively collaborating with the Scrum Master.[17] But the Scrum Master is an important partner for you, as I explain in this section.[18]

What the Scrum Master Should Do

The Scrum Master should take care of process, collaboration, and organisational change issues. This includes the following duties:

- *Staffing*: Help find people who have the right skills and are motivated to work on the product. For example, I've seen organisations where the Scrum Masters work with HR and the development team to find new team members.
- *Roles*: Ensure that the right roles are in place, their authority and responsibilities are clear, and everyone involved in the development effort understands them.
- *Process and collaboration*: Teach agile values, principles, and practices to the product person, development team, stakeholders, and management. Make sure that everyone understands the role they play, as mentioned earlier. Help people use the right processes in the right way. Encourage them to reflect on how they collaborate and discover ways to improve their work—for instance, through sprint retrospectives.
- *Meetings*: Prepare and facilitate meetings, including sprint planning, Daily Scrum, sprint review, and sprint retrospective. Establish ground rules. Ensure that everyone is heard and that nobody dominates or hijacks the meeting.

---

17 The Scrum Master role is part of the Scrum framework; see www.scrumguides.org.
18 In a traditional setting, a project manager or team lead supports the development teams, thereby helping product people to focus on their jobs. Please note, though, that a Scrum Master is *not* a project manager.

- *Productive work environment*: Help with setting up an environment that is conducive to creative teamwork—for instance, the right mix of open space and breakout rooms. Ensure that people have the infrastructure and tools they need to do a good job. This includes laptops, tablets, phones, and software tools, as well as a kitchen or coffee machine.
- *Organisational change*: Work with senior management, HR, and other business groups to implement the necessary organisational changes required to fully leverage agile practices and empower product people, possibly as part of an agile transformation or improvement program.

Having an effective Scrum Master allows you to focus on your job, and it avoids that you get too involved with people, process, and organisational issues. What's more, the Scrum Master can be a sparring partner for you—someone who you can discuss process and people questions and concerns with.

What the Scrum Master Should Not Do

In theory, your Scrum Master should focus on providing people and process leadership. In practice, however, Scrum Masters sometimes take on duties that do not belong to the role. These include the following roles:

- *Project management*: The Scrum Master is not a project manager. The individual should neither identify and assign tasks nor create reports like a release or sprint burndown chart. Instead, the person should teach the development team and you how to plan and track the progress of a sprint and release, respectively.
- *Product backlog work*: Keeping the product backlog up to date and in good shape is a responsibility the development team and you share. But it's not the job of the Scrum Master. You should therefore not expect that your Scrum Master refines the backlog for you. The individual is not a product backlog manager or a user story writer.

- *Team management:* The Scrum Master should not manage the development team. Instead, the individual should help the team practise self-organisation so that the members manage themselves.

You can view the Scrum Master as an enabler or a coach, someone who helps others understand how they can create a valuable product and continuously improve the way they work rather than doing the work for them.

Why You Shouldn't Take on Scrum Master Duties

Unfortunately, it's not uncommon in my experience that there is no Scrum Master at all or that the role is not effectively applied and not all the tasks listed previously are carried out. But as the Scrum Master work is important, someone else usually steps up and takes on the duties. Often, that's you, the person in charge of the product. While it's great to care about the development team and the process, taking on Scrum Master tasks in addition to your other work is a bad idea for the following three reasons:

First, taking on more duties is likely to make you overworked, which will reduce your creativity and affect your health. Alternatively, you may neglect some of your product responsibilities and sacrifice, for instance, carrying out continuous product discovery work.[19] Sadly, this usually creates more work for you in the future, as you desperately try to catch up with competitors or adjust to new trends.

Second, it takes time to acquire the necessary Scrum Master skills—think of facilitating organisational change or building productive teams, for instance. It's usually not something you can learn within

---

19 I use the term *product discovery* to refer to the work that determines if and why a new product should be developed and how an existing product can become or stay successful. This involves creating a brand-new product as well as enhancing an existing one. It includes strategy-related tasks, such as determining or adjusting the value proposition, target group, standout features, and business goals, as well as creating or updating a product roadmap that communicates how the strategy is likely to be implemented and how the product will probably develop, as I discuss in more detail in Pichler (2016, *Strategize*).

a few days or by attending a single training course. Consequently, I prefer to work with professional, full-time Scrum Masters who carry out their jobs for an extended period of time and are able to deepen their skills and develop the necessary expertise.

Third, if you seem to be able to carry out the Scrum Master tasks, then there is little need for your company to hire or develop Scrum Masters. Think about it: If management sees that you apparently cope without a Scrum Master, then why should they change anything? Therefore, *do not take on Scrum Master duties*—at least not for an extended period of time.

Shoot Your Scrum Master Troubles

I recently spoke to the COO of a company that creates learning apps about the product management challenges his company was experiencing. The individual was rather surprised when I pointed out to him that a likely cause of some of the issues was the complete lack of Scrum Masters. This shows that even nearly twenty years after the *"Manifesto for Agile Software Development"* (Beck et al. 2001) was published, the need for Scrum Masters, and agile coaches in general, is still not understood by every organisation that employs agile practices. If you are in a similar situation, explore how you can help the decision makers in your company understand that Scrum Masters are not optional but mandatory in order to establish an agile way of working and to support product people and their development teams. The same advice applies if your company employs the role but there aren't enough Scrum Masters to support you and your team. A little while ago, I spoke to a product person who had lost her Scrum Master, as the individual was needed to help set up another team. Consequently, she tried her best to cover the Scrum Master duties but unsurprisingly struggled with her workload. If there is no way that you can get a qualified Scrum Master, then consider if there are any consequences you should draw. I regard it as unfair to task someone with achieving product success but not to give the support the person needs. This does include a skilled Scrum Master who has enough availability.

If you are fortunate enough to have a Scrum Master, but the work of the individual is not effective, then explore its cause. Is your Scrum Master not knowledgeable or experienced enough? Do you find her or his advice unhelpful, or do you disagree with it? Or don't you get on with the individual? Don't you trust her or him? In either case, talk to the Scrum Master, preferably face to face. Share your observations, but make an effort to attentively listen to the person's perspective and empathise with her or him.[20] Offer your assistance when possible. For example, you might be able to help the individual attend a training course, assuming that's useful, of course. If you experience conflict, use the techniques discussed in the chapter *Conflict* in order to resolve the disagreement, strengthen the relationship, and build trust.

Guide the Development Team

The development team is a key partner for you, as the person in charge of the product: An effective dev team does not only design and implement the product, but its members also help you come up with and test new ideas, refine product backlog items, and make the right decisions. To reap these benefits, you must bring the right people together, give them the necessary guidance and support, and treat the development team as an equal partner.

Set the Team Up for Success

Development teams that aren't properly set up usually struggle to do a great job.[21] It's therefore useful to find the right people, ensure

---

20 I discuss having a difficult conversation with the Scrum Master in more detail in the chapter *Conversations*.

21 Hackman (2011, 149) suggests that the prep work, including finding the right members,

that the team has clear focus and ownership, and help create an environment that is conducive to teamwork. As Bill Campbell once said, "...leadership is about recognising that there's greatness in everyone, and your job is to create an environment where that greatness can emerge." (Cain 2017)

Give People a Choice

No matter what process and tools are used, it's the people who have the biggest impact on how successful a product will be: The latest agile and lean processes combined with the latest tools won't be of much help if the wrong people are on board. A great technique to find the right individuals is self-selection: Let people decide if they want to be on the team or not (Mamoli and Mole 2015). Consequently, the individuals are likely to be motivated to work on the product, which is a prerequisite for growing a great team and building a successful product. While self-selection has become popular in an agile context, it's not something new. For example, Smith and Reinertsen (1998, 123) write, "The importance of having team members volunteer for the project is often underestimated...When team members volunteer, they are psychologically more committed to the success of the team."

Organise around Products

When assembling a team, give people clear ownership. To do so, align teams with products: Every team should be responsible for a product or product part, like a feature. This helps create loosely coupled teams who are able to make progress with little or no dependencies to other teams—assuming that the products and their parts are loosely coupled too. In some cases, you may want to use architecture building blocks, such as the user interface or persistence layer, to form teams, which are also referred to as *component teams*. However, keep the number

---

determines up to 60 per cent how well a team will eventually perform.

of component teams small, particularly as long as you want to make bigger changes to your product. Component teams tend to have more interdependencies than *feature teams*—teams that are organised around features—which makes it harder to quickly validate ideas and to offer new or significantly enhanced functionality.

Ensure That the Team Members Have the Right Skills

Making sure that the individuals have the necessary skills when joining the team seems like a no-brainer. But in practice, that's not always the case in my experience. I once worked on a new voice-over IP phone where management added more people to the development effort in the hope of speeding up the progress. Unfortunately, none of the individuals possessed the relevant skills, and nobody had received any training up front. Needless to say, the development effort was significantly slowed down for a few months until the new team members were finally brought up to speed.

> **Cross-Functional versus Cross-Skilled**
>
> A cross-functional team has the skills required to provide a product, feature, or component. A cross-skilled team, however, consists of team members who have a broad skill set: In addition to having specialist skills, people also possess the necessary breadth of knowledge to work with another team member or to cover the individual's job, at least to a certain extent. For example, a user-experience designer might be able to help with testing, and a Java developer might be able to help with user-interface design or database programming. Cross-skilled teams tend to find it easier to plan and manage the work; they also tend to show better collaboration and exhibit stronger cohesion in my experience. If you believe that your development team would benefit from broadening their skill sets, then discuss the idea in one of the next sprint retrospectives.

The specific skills required will depend on the asset the development team looks after. For an end-user-facing product, this typically includes individuals with user-experience and user-interface design, architecture, programming, and testing skills. Agile development teams are therefore cross-functional: They contain all the capabilities required to provide a product or feature.

Form Stable Teams

Newly formed teams don't become productive overnight. It takes a while for a group of people to get to know each other, build trust, and be able to effectively collaborate.[22] What's more, every time a team changes, the team performance tends to dip: The new members have to get up to speed and familiarise themselves with the design and code, new connections have to be made, and new friendships have to be built. As Hackman (2011, 61) puts it, "teams with stable membership have healthier dynamics and perform better than those that constantly have to deal with the arrival of new members and the departure of veterans." You should therefore aim to create stable teams whose members work together for an extended period of time.

Consider Collocating the Team Members

While many organisations work with dispersed and distributed teams, my experience suggests that it is much harder to build trust when people don't have the opportunity to work face to face—despite the use of videoconferencing tools. I therefore recommend that you collocate team members at least temporarily whenever you work with a newly formed team or when you face a significant product challenge like creating a brand-new product or extending the life cycle of an existing one.

Help Create the Right Environment

I have seen more than one team tasked with developing a revenue-generating product but lacking basics like a joint workspace with whiteboards, decent machines, the right development tools, comfortable chairs, and a coffee machine. But having the right environment matters: It not only helps people be creative and productive but also shows the individuals that they are valued. While I view the Scrum Master as responsible for ensuring that the team members have an effective work

---

22 Different teambuilding models suggest the different stages groups have to pass through to gel and become productive. The Tuckman model, for example, suggests that teams have to go through a forming, storming, and norming stage before they are able to achieve their optimum productivity (Tuckman 1965).

environment, product people can often help influence the decision makers in the organisation and acquire a budget to create the right environment. If you are unsure whether your team has such an environment, ask the individuals in one of the next sprint retrospectives.

Let the Team Own the Solution

I commonly find that product people believe that they must precisely describe the product functionality and spoon-feed their development teams with detailed requirements. While this approach may be appropriate when a team does not sufficiently understand the user needs and lacks the skills to capture and refine requirements, it should not become the norm. Instead, you should empower your development team, help the members acquire the relevant knowledge, and allow people to take full ownership of the solution or, if that's not possible, the product details.

A great way to do this is to include the team members in product discovery and user experience work and allow them to directly observe and interact with users. This enables the development team to acquire the necessary knowledge and to influence product decisions. The former leverages the individuals' knowledge and creativity, which is likely to lead to better decisions; the latter will increase the team's motivation and strengthen their commitment. Additionally, involve the development team in the product backlog work and teach people, for example, how to formulate and refine user stories. This may increase your workload initially. But in the long run, it will reward you with a more autonomous and motivated team, less time spent on breaking down requirements and answering questions during the sprint, and more time to take care of product strategy and discovery.

My Team Insists on Receiving Detailed Requirements

A common objection I hear when I talk to product people about helping their development team to become self-sufficient and be able to take on more responsibility is that the team isn't willing to do so. Instead, the team members insist that the product person provides them with detailed requirements so that they can focus on implementing the solution.

If that's the case for you, then I recommend that you use one of the upcoming retrospectives to understand why people have this expectation. In my experience, there are two common reasons: a misunderstanding of what agile development teams are supposed to do and a fear of punishment.

Sometimes developers haven't been taught that being a member of an agile team is different from writing code in a traditional environment. Members of agile teams are granted more ownership and freedom. But they are required to accept the responsibility that comes with it and to take on additional tasks, such as working on the product backlog and creating and refining user stories.

The second cause is often harder to address: If developers were reprimanded or felt disadvantaged in the past when they showed initiative, then they are likely to resist taking on more responsibilities, and they might only carry out the work stated in their job descriptions. Building trust will help the individuals open up and take on more ownership.

Don't Manage the Team

A common mistake I see product people make is to manage an agile development team—for example, assist the team members to identify tasks, track progress within a sprint, or help resolve disagreements between team members. While it's great to care about people, you should manage your product, not the team. An agile development team should be self-organising: The members have a joint responsibility for determining how much work can be done in a given period of time, identifying the specific tasks that have to be carried out, deciding who does what and how people collaborate, designing and implementing the product, and tracking the work progress. Frameworks like Scrum and Kanban support self-organisation by offering specific practices and tools, like sprint planning, Daily Scrums or stand-up meetings, and sprint backlogs or Kanban boards. In simple terms, the development team should own and manage the work required to turn product backlog items into shippable software. In Scrum, the team owns what happens in a sprint; in Kanban, the team owns the work on the Kanban board.[23]

That's at least the theory. In practice, teams sometimes struggle to effectively manage their work. Imagine that your development team is not making enough progress in the current sprint. Realising that the sprint goal is under threat, you are getting increasingly worried. The team, however, does not seem to be concerned. What should you do? Before I suggest an answer, let me first state what you should *not* do: You should neither suppress your concerns nor tell the team what they have to do. If you are genuinely concerned about the progress, then it is only right to share your perspective with the development team in an appropriate way. It might be that the individuals are so busy designing, coding, and testing the product that they have lost track of the overall progress. However, stepping in, telling people what's wrong and how to solve it, is something you should refrain from doing. As mentioned before, it's the team's responsibility to own and manage the work in the sprint, not yours. This includes identifying and addressing progress issues.

How can you then share your perspective and help the team? My suggestion is to talk to the team, for instance, at the end of a Daily Scrum, and to ask people if they are happy with the sprint progress. That's often enough to raise the team's awareness and to help people realise that there is an issue. But if it isn't sufficient, share your view and explain why you are concerned. For example, you might say that for the third day in a row, the sprint burndown has been flat and that you are worried that the team may not be able to meet the sprint goal. But leave it up to the team to decide what to do with the information. Most likely, the individuals will either realise that there is a problem or explain to you that your concerns are invalid and that everything is under control. If, however, you disagree with the team's perspective and believe that the sprint goal will be missed, you

---

23 With the exception of the input column, assuming that it contains (a subset of) the product backlog.

should still not interfere but allow the team to take full responsibility for the sprint. Then hold the team accountable at the end of the sprint and provide constructive but honest feedback. Investigate what went wrong in the sprint retrospective to avoid a similar issue from occurring again. Note that becoming a self-organising team takes time and requires support, particularly for newly formed groups. Having a Scrum Master on board who can help the team self-organise is particularly valuable at this stage.

Should Product People Attend the Daily Scrum?

While the Scrum framework's advice has changed over the years, I find that attending the Daily Scrum at least twice a week is usually beneficial: It allows you to see what's happening in the current sprint and to understand if there is anything you can do to help the development team. You may find, for example, that some user stories are done and are waiting to be reviewed by you, or you may discover that the team is struggling with a user story and requires your help.

But be careful not to interfere with the work of the team, as previously pointed out. The Daily Scrum is a meeting for the development team. Its purpose is to help people organise their work. It's not a status meeting or a workshop where problems are solved. If you find that the team members report their progress to you or expect you to tell them what to do, then the team is not yet self-organising and seems to regard you as a project manager or team leader. Share your observations with the team and consider not attending the meeting for the remainder of the sprint. Use the next sprint retrospective to discuss how the meeting is used and how to make it more effective.

Effectively Interact with the Development Team

If an agile development team is self-managing, how can you then guide its members? The answer to this question depends on the development process used. It differs from, say, Scrum to Kanban and Extreme Programming. As Scrum continues to be the most popular agile development framework at the time of writing, I focus on it in this section. If you use a different development framework, then choose the recommendations that work for you.

Get the Product Backlog Ready and Collaboratively Decide on the Sprint Goal

Ensure that the product backlog is ready for sprint planning.[24] This is best done by refining the product backlog items together with the team. Additionally, jointly set the sprint goal. Each sprint should have an objective that describes the sprint's desired outcome, the reason for carrying out the sprint. The team should be reasonably happy with the goal and consider it to be meaningful and realistic. Therefore, don't push your sprint goal on to the team. Instead, look for an inclusive, agreeable solution using the techniques described in the chapter *Decision-Making and Negotiation.*

Respect the Team's Right to Determine the Workload

Allow the team to freely determine how much work can be done in a sprint. Do not pressure people, and do not try to force more work on the development team. Agile teams are empowered to determine their own workload, which results in motivated, committed teams and realistic goals. Additionally, it achieves a sustainable pace that is conducive to creative work and does not impact people's health.

If you ask people to carry out more work than they can realistically cope with, the team members may become demotivated and start to take shortcuts, like compromising quality and neglecting documentation. In the worst case, people will leave or fall ill: I have met a number of people, for instance, who suffered heart attacks and slipped discs caused by the high stress levels they experienced while developing software. Sustainable pace wants to prevent this from happening.[25]

---

24 Such a backlog is prioritised, and it contains enough detailed, high-priority items to support the next sprint.

25 The *"Manifesto for Agile Software Development"* (Beck et al. 2001) states as one of its twelve principles, "Agile processes promote sustainable development. The sponsors, developers, and users should be able to maintain a constant pace indefinitely."

Make Time to Interact with the Team

Be available to answer questions from the team during the sprint in order to help them make progress and to provide feedback on work results. If you are not available or difficult to reach, people might get fed up with trying to get hold of you or waiting for an answer. Instead, they might just go ahead and make the necessary decisions without your input. By the same token, don't spend too much time with the team. Otherwise, you might neglect strategic product management tasks, such as tracking the product performance, keeping an eye on the competition, and talking to users and customers.

If you find that the team's demand on your time is too big, raise the issue in the next sprint retrospective. Get the team members' views and search for a solution together. It might include increasing the involvement of the team members in the backlog work, providing the team with the big-picture knowledge mentioned earlier, or further detailing the high-priority product backlog items before they are pulled into a sprint.

Hold People Accountable

Provide clear feedback on the work of the team and hold people accountable for reaching the sprint goal, assuming that it was collaboratively decided and that the team could freely determine the workload. Be respectful and honour the team members' effort and goodwill. Recognise that software development is challenging. Despite people's best intentions, things go wrong. For instance, tasks are missed in sprint planning, a piece of technology does not work as expected, or the development environment is unstable, to name just a few common problems.

But do not accept that a team routinely overcommits: If your team can freely determine the workload, then people have to learn to get their forecasts right—they are responsible for getting the work done.[26] If you work with a team that regularly fails to meet the sprint goal, then do not ignore the issue but address it in the next sprint

---

26 Scrum suggests that as soon as a team discovers that there is too much work to be completed in a sprint, its members talk to the product owner to discuss how to proceed and which items should be finished.

retrospective. To effectively bring your message across, avoid harsh speech and consider using such techniques as *positive first* and *flipping* and *framing*, which I discuss in the chapter *Conversations*.

Participate in the Retrospectives

Last but not least, actively participate in sprint retrospectives. It is important for you to regularly attend this meeting for two reasons: First, you can often contribute to resolving an issue. Second, you understand why it is necessary that the team dedicates time in the next sprint to solve an issue. Don't be a bystander in the meeting. Instead, share your perspective and contribute to identifying issues and their causes and determining actionable improvements. Use the meeting to raise concerns—for example, regularly missing the sprint goal—and to receive feedback on your own work—for instance, ask the team members if they are happy with their involvement in the product backlog work. But do not dominate or take over the meeting.[27]

How Do I Know That My Team Is Doing a Good Job?

Formally speaking, a development team in Scrum does a good job if the team is able to reliably meet the agreed sprint goals and to deliver product increments that offer a great user experience and exhibit the desired software quality.[28] But there is more to it. To be able to do a good job for an extended period of time, your team should also be *healthy*.

Such a team is characterised by frequent and ad hoc interactions in a sprint. This includes meetings everyone participates in, people helping each other complete tasks, and the entire team occasionally having coffee or lunch together. But if there is an awkward atmosphere in the meetings, if people don't contribute much or only one or two individuals speak, or if the same conflict keeps recurring, your team is probably not doing great. Similarly, if team members don't work together, have limited interactions during the sprint, and focus on their individual tasks, something is not right.

---

27 As mentioned earlier, it's the Scrum Master's job to prepare and facilitate the retrospective, thereby ensuring that everybody participates and no one dominates.

28 The "Definition of Done" in Scrum captures the quality criteria a product has to fulfil; see www.scrumguides.org.

If you believe that your team is unhealthy, share your perspective in the next retrospective. Don't ignore the issue, hoping it will go away on its own—it most likely won't. But don't jump in and fix things for the team: A self-organising team has to learn to resolve collaboration issues. Additionally, talk to the Scrum Master, understand her or his perspective, and ask the individual what she or he intends to do.

If conflicts persist despite help from a qualified Scrum Master, then it might be best to suggest adjusting the team composition. This can be helpful if the initial team setup was not right, be it that the personalities are not compatible or the people's skills don't complement each other. I've also seen Scrum Masters tell a team member who continued to show disruptive behaviour to leave the team. However, none of these changes should be forced on to the team. Instead, the entire team should look for a solution that ideally works for everyone. This creates transparency, gives people the opportunity to contribute, and reduces the risk that some individuals end up frustrated or feeling treated unfairly.

Give the Team Time to Experiment and Learn

Imagine that your product is doing really well. The users love it, and the business is reaping its benefits. But if the development team is so busy cranking out new features and enhancements that its members don't have the time and capacity to look into new technologies and enhance their skills, then you run the risk of getting caught out and overtaken by your competitors in the not-too-distant future.

Think about it like this: Software development—much like product management—is similar to riding a bicycle. When I ride my bike, I focus on the here and now, and I look ahead at the same time. The former involves keeping the bike balanced, evenly turning the cranks, and choosing the right gear. The latter means seeing where the road or trail is heading so that I can adjust in time and, for example, turn the bike to the left or right, break, or avoid an obstacle. When you manage your product, you should do the same: You should engage in enough discovery and strategy work to see things coming and to make the right choices. At the same time, you need to pay attention to the product details to offer enough guidance to your team and to collect the relevant data.

The same is true for a development team: People require enough time to look ahead, to learn new skills, and to experiment with new technologies and tools. Otherwise your development team risks "crashing." For example, its members may have overlooked new technologies, which are now exploited by a competitor; the software architecture can no longer support adding more users; the code base has become hard to change; and creating new features takes an increasingly long time. You should therefore give the team enough room to experiment with new ideas and acquire new knowledge. Some teams use gold cards to allocate time in a sprint for experimentation and learning; others use hack days or benefit from the 20 per cent rule made popular by Google. Whatever works for your team, help people look ahead and prepare for the future. This will benefit your product, and it will have a positive impact on team morale.

Should Product People Have Technical Skills?

If you manage a digital product that end users employ, such as a web or mobile app, then you usually do not require in-depth technical skills, such as being able to program in Java and write SQL code. But if you look after a technical product that is integrated into a larger offering—for instance, an internal platform that provides shared assets—then you will require the appropriate technical skills in order to talk to the users, who are likely to be developers; formulate technical requirements; and define software interfaces (APIs).

Independent of your specific product job, you should take an interest in software technology and be aware of major trends. At the time of writing, these include machine learning (ML) and Internet of Things (IoT). Additionally, you will benefit from having a basic understanding of core concepts, like software architecture design patterns and agile development practices—for example, test-driven development and continuous integration. This knowledge helps you empathise and communicate with the development team. It allows you to better understand some of the challenges the team members experience.

Make sure, though, that you leave it up to the team to make the right technical decisions. Don't tell people what to do—which can be tempting for product people with strong technical skills. If you feel that people lack the necessary capabilities, discuss your observation with the team in the next sprint retrospective and jointly determine the right improvement measures.

Lead the Stakeholders

As the person in charge of the product, your job is not to please or satisfy the stakeholders. Instead, you should lead the way and pro-actively guide the individuals to ensure that your product creates the desired value for the users and business.

Involve the Right People

To get started, reflect on who the stakeholders of your product are. Generally speaking, a stakeholder is anyone who has a stake in your product, who is affected by it, or who shows an interest in the offering. While this definition includes customers and users, I use the term in this book to refer to the *internal business stakeholders*. These are the individuals whose help you need to provide the product. For example, the stakeholders for a commercial product are likely to include representatives from marketing, sales, and support. But you may also engage people from legal and finance. For an in-house product, your stakeholders may be the business units that will use the product as well as operations/IT.

Once you have identified the stakeholders, you can take the next step and determine how to engage the individuals. A handy tool for this is the *power-interest grid*, described in Ackermann and Eden (2011). As its name suggests, the grid analyses the stakeholders by taking into account their power and interest; it assumes that people take a low or high interest in your product and have low or high power. This results in four stakeholder groups: players, subjects, context setters, and crowd, as figure 2 shows. To find out how much a stakeholder is likely to be interested in your product, consider if and to which extent the person will be affected by it. To understand how powerful a stake-holder is, ask yourself if you need the individual to develop or provide the product and if the individual can influence product decisions.

Stakeholders with high interest and high power are called *players*. These individuals are important partners for you. Consequently, you should establish a trustful relationship with them, create shared goals, and involve them in important product decisions.

```
                  ┌──────────────┬──────────────┐
         HIGH INTEREST           │              │
                  │ SUBJECTS     │ PLAYERS      │
                  │ Involve      │ Collaborate  │
                  │              │              │
                  ├──────────────┼──────────────┤
         LOW INTEREST            │ CONTEXT      │
                  │ CROWD        │ SETTERS      │
                  │ Inform       │ Consult      │
                  │              │              │
                  └──────────────┴──────────────┘
                    LOW POWER      HIGH POWER
```

Figure 2: *Power-Interest Grid*

Subjects are individuals with high interest but low power—for example, product people and development teams who work on related products. These individuals are affected by the product and may be keen to influence it, but they can't veto or change decisions. Subjects can make great allies who can help you secure understanding and buy-in for your product across the business. Keep them involved by aligning product roadmaps and inviting them to bigger sprint review meetings, for instance.

People with low interest but high power are called *context setters*. They affect the product's context, but they take little interest in the product itself. Context setters are often powerful senior and executive managers. Regularly consult them to build and maintain a healthy relationship, but don't allow the context setters to dictate decisions. Attentively listen to what they have to say and empathise with them, but have the courage to decline their suggestions and requests if they are not helpful to create value for the users and business. Remember: Your job is not to please the stakeholders but to achieve product success.[29]

---

29 I share tips on how to best say no in the chapter *Conversations*.

Everyone else is part of the *crowd*. As these individuals are not particularly interested in your product and don't have the power to influence product decisions, it's usually sufficient to keep them informed; give them access to the product's wiki website, for instance, or update them on significant product strategy and roadmap changes.

Helping Stakeholders Move into the Right Quadrant

While the power-interest grid is a neat tool to group stakeholders, the individuals don't always act as you expect based on the quadrant to which they belong. Some people want to contribute more and have a greater say in product decisions than you think they should; others do not want to be involved as much as you would like them to be. To help stakeholders move into the right quadrant, try the following tips:

Assuming that you have assigned the person to the right group, talk to the individual and explore why she or he wants to be more or less involved. In the former case, the person might not trust the other players to make the right decisions: The individual might be concerned that the decisions will negatively affect her or him, or the person might want to make sure that her or his interests are taken into account. In the latter case, the stakeholder might not have enough time to be more involved; the individual might dislike some of the other players or have experienced issues in the past when working with them; or the individual might worry about experiencing a disadvantage, like being held accountable for the decisions when things go wrong.[30]

Once you've carefully listened to the individual, consider how you can help the stakeholder. If it's a trust issue, you might want to offer involving the person in larger product strategy reviews or better aligning product and business strategy, for example. If it's an availability issue, you might want to clarify how much of the individual's time will actually be required or ask the person what you can do to help the stakeholder free up more time, for instance.

Build a Stakeholder Community

I often see the product person interact with the stakeholders individually, going from stakeholder to stakeholder and trying to convince or persuade the individual to agree to a plan or to negotiate with her or him. While this approach can work, it has a number of drawbacks.

---

30   If you find that an individual wants to be more involved in order to share her or his expertise and help, then this may indicate that your initial stakeholder analysis was not correct: The individual may be a *player* rather than a *subject*.

First, the individual stakeholders are often not aware of their respective needs and concerns, as the person in charge of the product communicates with the individuals on a one-on-one basis. This tends to lead to a lack of understanding and trust amongst the stakeholders. Second, the collective wisdom and creativity of the group stays untapped: Novel ideas often emerge when people come together and engage in open, constructive discussion. Third, if there is no sense of togetherness amongst the stakeholders, it will be difficult to establish shared goals to which the individuals feel committed. Aligning the stakeholders may consequently feel like herding cats, with every stakeholder going off in a separate direction and pursuing her or his individual interests. In the worst case, the product person ends up as a go-between, tries to broker a deal between the stakeholders, and negotiates a weak compromise, which is hardly a recipe for achieving product success.

Instead of interacting with the players on a one-on-one basis, aim to build a stakeholder community whose members work together for an extended period of time and who learn to trust, respect, and support each other. In other words, move from stakeholder management to stakeholder collaboration.

Form a Stable Group

Assuming that you have the right players on board, keep the group stable: Minimise any changes to the group and ask people to work with you for an extended period of time. As explained earlier, this is necessary so that people can get to know each other, learn to understand and trust one another, and establish shared values and norms, which are prerequisites for effective collaboration. Additionally, it makes your life easier, as you don't have to repeatedly phase in new people and introduce them to the product and its context. It would be undesirable, for instance, to have the marketing group send a new representative every time a strategy workshop takes place. Instead, one marketer should represent marketing. A group that experiences frequent changes suffers from limited trust and low productivity in my experience.

Practise Collaborative Goal Setting

A great way to foster mutual understanding and to align people is to jointly set goals. This might initially be challenging, as the stakeholders may have to get to know each other before they are able to trust and respect one another. You might also have to deal with vocal individuals or powerful stakeholders who might want to see their ideas and needs met. But once people have accepted common ground rules and learnt how collaborative decision-making works, collaboration will become easier and more effective. Please refer to the chapter *Goals* for more information on identifying the right goals and the chapter *Decision-Making and Negotiation* for techniques to decide together.

Create Clear Roles and Responsibilities

While you want people to support each other and work towards shared goals, it is helpful for everyone to understand what the group members' roles and responsibilities are. If people aren't clear on what is expected of them and who is doing what, confusion arises and collaboration becomes more difficult. A simple exercise to help people develop this understanding is to create a one-page description of each role. State the role name, authority and responsibility, and main tasks. Then jointly review the descriptions; clarify any questions and address any issues. Don't forget to review and update the role descriptions once in a while to ensure that they stay helpful.

Bring People Together

Learning to effectively collaborate is difficult when people work in different locations and are unable to be in the same room. While video calls are great to exchange information, they are less effective in my experience to build trust, develop empathy, and agree on how to best work together. I therefore recommend that you collocate the players—at least temporarily, say, for two weeks—in order to build a stakeholder community. You can accelerate this process by carrying out specific teambuilding activities and spending time together outside the office. Additionally, consider having joint onsite meetings at least once per quarter to renew and strengthen the connections between the individuals.

Hold Retrospectives

A great way to improve the collaboration between the players and to address any issues and problems is to regularly carry out a stakeholder retrospective, for example, once per month. Determine issues, analyse them, and identify specific improvement measures, similar to what you do in a sprint retrospective. Encourage people to be honest and open, but refrain from blaming others, assigning fault, and using harsh speech. Don't be afraid to show vulnerability and admit to mistakes. This is a sign of strength, not weakness; it will encourage others to follow your lead and help you find ways to improve things.

Engage the Scrum Master

Building a stakeholder community while managing the product and collaborating with the development team can be a lot of work. To avoid becoming overworked or neglecting your core product management responsibilities, ask the Scrum Master to help with establishing the community. Ask the individual to advise and support you; help create ground rules; support the creation of role descriptions; facilitate meetings so that nobody dominates and everybody is heard; and tackle any organisational impediments you might bump against, for example, insufficient travel budget to have face-to-face meetings.

Collaborating with Other Product People

Working with other product people comes in two flavours: The individuals may be stakeholders, or they may share product ownership with you. In the former instance, the person may be in charge of another product you have to coordinate with. Think of an app within the same product portfolio that offers a similar user experience or shared features or a platform your product is built on. If that's the case, engage the individuals in the same way as you involve other subjects, and align the product roadmaps.

In the second case, the other product people will manage the product together with you. Assuming that you are the person in charge of the overall product, they might own product parts—for example, features like registration and search—or components and architecture building blocks, like a collection of micro services or a persistence layer.[31] No matter how you divide the work, make sure that you establish a trustful connection with the individuals and involve them in decisions that affect them. Additionally, help them do a great job, for example, by mentoring and coaching them, if necessary, and giving them the authority they need.

Involve the Individuals in Product Discovery and Strategy Work

I am a big fan of involving the players early on in the process of developing a brand-new product or a life-cycle extension. Invite the stakeholders, together with development team members, to a kick-off workshop to create a product vision and initial product strategy. Ask the individuals to help you validate the strategy and to find a workable business model, as I describe in more detail in Pichler (2016, *Strategize*). This may include joint user research like observing and interviewing users or carrying out due diligence work to select the right partner or supplier. Then take the next step and detail the overall product strategy in the form of a product roadmap that contains shared goals, as I explain in the chapter *Goals*.

Additionally, involve the players in continuous discovery and strategy work. This may comprise jointly reviewing the product performance using the appropriate key performance indicators (KPIs); exploring new market trends, including appropriate technology, regulatory, or social changes; analysing the competition; considering relevant developments at your own company, like changes in the business strategy; reviewing and adjusting the product roadmap; and brainstorming new features and discussing feature requests. A great way to carry out the work is to run collaborative strategy reviews once per quarter, as a rule of thumb.

Bringing the players together allows you to leverage their expertise and creativity; creates a shared understanding and helps the

---

31 I discuss different strategies to scale product ownership and jointly manage a larger product in Pichler (2016, "Scaling the Product Owner Role").

individuals acquire relevant knowledge about the users and customers; increases the chances that the stakeholders will support the strategic decisions and buy into the appropriate goals; and last but not least, helps you build and strengthen the stakeholder community. This in turn makes stakeholder alignment significantly easier: When people support common goals, they are aligned.

Engage the Key Stakeholders in Product Development Work

Involving the players in discovery and strategy work is great, but it is not enough. Imagine that the stakeholders have developed a validated product strategy and actionable roadmap together with you, and you now continue to progress the product together with the development team. How do you then keep the players informed? Personally, I would not want to rely on status reports, which people might ignore or misunderstand. Instead, invite the players to attend the sprint review meetings in Scrum and operations meetings in Kanban at least once per month, as a rule of thumb. This allows the individuals to see for themselves how the product is progressing, offer their feedback, and share any concerns, thereby making it more likely to create a product that can be effectively marketed, sold, serviced, and operated.

Be careful, though, not to blindly accept any stakeholder requests. Be grateful for any ideas and suggestions, but evaluate them in the context of the product strategy and roadmap. If the request does not help you to move closer to the agreed goals, and if there is not a clear case for changing them, then kindly but firmly decline the request. But make an effort to listen with an open mind. Try to understand why someone wants a new feature added, for example. Maybe it's neither desirable nor possible to include the feature right now. But perhaps there is another way to meet the person's underlying need. What's more, when people don't feel heard and understood, when you don't empathise with them, they will find it hard to accept no as an answer.

My Stakeholders Don't Want to Attend Sprint Review Meetings

In theory, Scrum expects that the players regularly attend the sprint review meeting. This ensures that everyone understands the progress made and has the opportunity to voice ideas and concerns. In practice, however, not all stakeholders are enthusiastic about regularly attending review meetings. If that's the case for you, then find out why the individuals are hesitant to participate: Are they concerned about further increasing their workload? Does the meeting not provide enough value for them? Do they not fully understand why they are needed or how they can effectively contribute? Have they had bad experiences—for example, did they feel ignored, misunderstood, or criticised? Next, explore how you can help. Consider involving the Scrum Master, for instance, to adjust the ground rules used in the meeting or to explain how an agile development process works and why active stakeholder participation is important.

Don't Tolerate Inappropriate Behaviour

Leading the stakeholders commonly includes addressing issues—for example, a stakeholder does not feel accountable for a shared decision and consequently fails to implement it. If that's the case, don't be afraid to remind the individual of the shared agreement and her or his accountability. Assuming that some form of consensus was achieved, you should expect the person to follow through with the decision. It is not acceptable in my mind when a stakeholder intentionally acts against a joint decision or common goal. Similarly, don't allow individuals to use a personal conversation with you to make requests, like adding a new feature. If this happens, ask people to attend the appropriate meeting and to share their request with the other stakeholders. This creates transparency, fosters joint ownership, and avoids the impression that you might favour certain individuals. Finally, don't put up with inappropriate communication behaviour, like blaming others, bending the truth, and intentionally dominating the conversation. Ask people to treat each other with respect even if there is conflict, avoid harsh and false speech, and attentively listen to one another. Be a role model and reflect on your own speaking and listening habits.[32]

---

32   I discuss listening and speaking in more detail in the chapter *Conversations*.

Whenever you are faced with unhelpful behaviour from stakeholders, do not ignore the issue, but tackle it. As suggested before, listen to the individual's perspective with an open mind, empathise with the stakeholder, and explore the person's needs and interests along the lines discussed in the chapter *Conflict*. But ensure that the individual understands the impact of her or his behaviour and kindly but firmly request that the stakeholder act in the best interest of the users and business. Untreated people problems seldom go away on their own; they usually grow bigger—like mushrooms in the dark. And if you tolerate inappropriate behaviour, other stakeholders are likely to believe that acting improperly is acceptable.

If you find that a stakeholder repeatedly and knowingly goes against a group decision, and if you have talked to the individual and tried to amicably resolve the issue, consider asking the person to leave the group. This may require a conversation with the line manager of the individual, your manager, and the sponsor of the product. Whatever the right way forward is, do not put up with toxic behaviour, and don't shy away from conflict. As with other people issues, you may want to involve the Scrum Master to help you address the problem.[33]

---

33   I offer advice on constructively dealing with conflict in the chapter *Conflict*.

GOALS

If you want to build a ship, don't drum up the men to gather wood,
divide the work, and give orders. Instead, teach them to yearn for the vast and endless sea.
Antoine de Saint-Exupéry

Goals are key to effectively guide the development team and stakeholders: When applied correctly, they establish a shared purpose, ensure that their efforts are aligned, and provide the individuals with the necessary autonomy to do their work. This chapter introduces a set of product-centric, cascading goals as well as guidelines to help you create the right goals.

A Chain of Goals

Over the years, I have experimented with different goals to advance products while at the same time aligning development team members and stakeholders. This has led me to propose the chain of goals shown in *figure 3*.

The goals in figure 3 are linked. They form a chain with progressively refined goals: The product vision helps you discover the right user and business goals, the user and business goals help you determine the right product goals, and the product goals should help you identify the right sprint goals. This way, the vision is indirectly connected to each sprint goal and vice versa. What's more, every sprint goal should be a step towards a product goal, every product goal should help you reach a user or business goal, and the user and business goals should bring you closer to your vision. As a consequence, changes in lower-level goals can trigger adjustments in higher-level ones. For example, if the development team fails to reach a sprint goal, then this might have an impact on the next product goal. This might even cause a change in the user or business goal. And if you weren't able to find an effective product strategy with user and business goals that can be reached, then you should consider changing the product vision. Therefore, make sure that you regularly review your goals and keep them in sync—for example, in product strategy meetings and product backlog refinement sessions. Let's now take a closer look at the goals in figure 3.

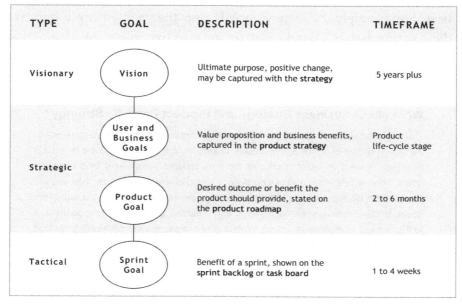

TYPE	GOAL	DESCRIPTION	TIMEFRAME
Visionary	Vision	Ultimate purpose, positive change, may be captured with the **strategy**	5 years plus
Strategic	User and Business Goals	Value proposition and business benefits, captured in the **product strategy**	Product life-cycle stage
	Product Goal	Desired outcome or benefit the product should provide, stated on the **product roadmap**	2 to 6 months
Tactical	Sprint Goal	Benefit of a sprint, shown on the **sprint backlog** or **task board**	1 to 4 weeks

Figure 3: *A Chain of Goals for Product People*

Product Vision

The first and possibly most powerful goal in figure 3 is the product vision. It describes the ultimate reason for creating a product and the positive change it should bring about. A sample vision I like to use is *healthy eating*. As this example shows, the vision is best captured as a brief statement or slogan. What's more, an effective vision inspires people; it provides a motivation for working on the product. By the same token, it can also help you decide if you should work on a product or not. Life is too short to work on a product you don't find meaningful.

As the vision is an inspirational and visionary goal, it cannot be measured. In fact, you might never fully realise your vision. That's OK, as long as it acts as the product's true north, providing continued guidance for everyone involved in developing and providing the product. The vision should therefore cover at least the next five years. Additionally, keep your vision free of any solution-specific information. For example, "Create a mobile app that helps people improve their eating habits" would not be an effective vision. A vision that is not tied to a product idea will allow you to pivot, to change your strategy while staying grounded in your vision.

What about Business Strategy and Product Portfolio Strategy?

You might be wondering how the business and product portfolio strategy relate to the goals shown in figure 3. My answer is simple: You typically require at least a business strategy in order to choose the right product vision, user, and business goals.[34] If your product is part of a portfolio, a group of related products, then you will benefit from having a product portfolio strategy available to select the appropriate goals. In other words, your vision, user, and business goals, should be connected to the product portfolio or business strategy. Otherwise, you risk pursuing goals that might not benefit the product portfolio or company.

---

34   Lafley and Martin (2013) suggest that a business strategy should cover the company's vision; the markets to be served; the competitive advantage; the capabilities required, including new and changed products; and the management systems that are needed.

User and Business Goals

The user and business goals in figure 3 are strategic goals that are derived from the vision. They form part of the product strategy, which describes the approach you intend to use to move towards the vision.[35] A user goal describes the problem users want to see addressed, for example, lose weight, or the benefit people want to gain, for instance, reduce the risk of developing type 2 diabetes.[36] Compare this to a business goal, which states the benefits the company developing and providing the product wants to achieve, for instance, diversify the business, open up a new revenue stream, or develop the main brand.

Whatever user and business goals you choose, make sure that they are specific and measurable. This allows you to select the right key performance indicators (KPIs) and understand if your product is meeting its goals. Additionally, be aware that the goals are tied to the life-cycle stage of your product—like the entire product strategy. For instance, if your product currently is in the introduction stage, then the product strategy with the user and business goals should be focused on achieving product-market fit and entering the growth stage. Once this has been achieved, you will have to update or rework your strategy, user, and business goals: The mainstream users typically have different expectations compared to the early market, and some of the business goals may change too. Profitability, for example, is a goal that is typically not available before a product has entered the growth stage. Unlike the vision, user and business goals will therefore change as your product develops and matures and, by doing so, encounters new challenges.

---

35 Additional elements of a product strategy include the target group, the market or market segment you want to address, and the product's stand-out features; see Pichler (2016, *Strategize*). If you use my *Product Vision Board* to formulate the product vision and strategy, then the user goals would be captured in the needs section. You can hence think of the user goals as user needs. You can download the Product Vision Board for free from my website, www.romanpichler.com.

36 You might be wondering where the customer goals are. I have intentionally omitted them for the sake of simplicity. If your customers are distinct from your users, then you should also identify and state customer goals.

Chicken and Egg

I often get asked what should come first, user or business goals. My answer is: Start with the users and their needs. Once you clearly understand why people would want to use the product, what job it should do for them, which problem it should solve, or which benefit it should create, consider how you can create value for the business. Only if your product has a compelling value proposition will you be able to find a viable business model. Additionally, if you start with business goals, you risk prioritising the business needs over the user goals. In the worst case, this leads to unethical product decisions that might harm the users.

Product Goals

With the user and business goals in place, you can take the next step and determine the right product goals. Each product goal should be a step towards meeting a user or business goal and describe specific benefits, such as acquire users, increase engagement, generate revenue, or remove technical debt to future-proof the product. To determine the right product goals, ask yourself how you can meet the user and business goals in the product strategy. What is the best way to achieve them? How can you break them down into smaller, intermediate, measurable goals? While product goals are strategic in nature, they are more specific than user and business goals. Additionally, they cover a shorter timeframe, typically between two and six months. Consequently, they are great to direct and align the work of the development team and stakeholders.[37]

Note that your product goals are not fixed, but they may change. You may find, for instance, that the development progress is slower than anticipated or that the product goal is too ambitious. In both cases, you will have to adjust the objective. I like to capture product goals on the product roadmap together with their metrics, and I have a preference to work with a goal-oriented roadmap, like my

---

37   If you work with major releases or product versions, then you can determine a specific product goal for each release or version. For example, version 3 has the goal to acquire more users, and version 3.5 should increase conversion.

GO Product Roadmap, which you can download for free from my website, www.romanpichler.com.

Sprint Goal

The last goal in the chain in figure 3 is the sprint goal. A sprint goal states the desired outcome of a sprint—for example, find out if users are willing to share personal information before they start using the app, test integration with leading smart scales, or finish the dashboard in order to release a first version to the test group and learn how people respond to it. Make sure that your sprint goals state the reason for running a sprint, like acquiring new knowledge, addressing a risk, or providing a benefit to users, and avoid listing product backlog items, which is a common mistake in my experience. Each sprint goal should be a step towards the next product goal, and it covers the next one to four weeks. It is therefore a tactical, short-term goal.

I find it helpful to state the sprint goal on the sprint backlog or task board so that it is visible and reminds the development team of the shared short-term goal they have committed themselves to. If your team works with Kanban, then it might still be helpful to agree on weekly goals that direct the work of the team members—something you may want to discuss with the team. Similarly, if you currently employ Scrum but don't use sprint goals, consider experimenting with them. A sprint goal aligns the development team members, encourages close collaboration, and makes it easier to determine the success of the sprint.

Make Your Goals Great

While I do hope that you will find the goals just discussed helpful, you must decide, of course, if they are right for your product and organisation. Whichever goals you choose to use, apply the following criteria to ensure that your goals are effective:

- *Shared*: If you want people to take ownership of goals and feel responsible for reaching them, you should ensure that the goals are shared. This is best done by actively involving the individuals in choosing the goals, as I explain in more detail later in this chapter. If that's not possible—for example, as someone could not attend the meeting where the decision was taken, or the individual joined the product development effort at a later stage—explain to the person why the goal was chosen and patiently address any questions or concerns.

- *Realistic*: All your goals—apart from visionary ones—should be achievable and measurable. Goals that are overly ambitious can demotivate people and encourage unhealthy work practices like working excessive overtime. I'll say more about setting realistic goals later in this chapter.

- *Inspirational*: Good goals create a natural pull, and people should want to work on them. That's particularly true for overarching goals like the product vision. To establish such goals, focus on the desired outcome rather than on the output, and consider the benefit you would like to create or the problem you would like to address. Additionally, involve people in choosing the goals, as mentioned earlier, and choose ethical goals, as I discuss later in this chapter.

- *Alignment creating*: Effective goals direct people and help ensure that their work results create the desired outcome. This implies that the goals are clearly understood by everyone.

- *Autonomy fostering*: While creating alignment is important, you don't want to micromanage people. Good goals therefore give the development team and stakeholders the freedom to figure out what they need to do. Think of a sprint goal, allowing the team to decide what needs to be done in a sprint and how the work should be achieved, for example.

- *Holistic and systematically linked*: Make sure that your goals cover product vision, strategy, and tactics and that they systematically connect with higher-level goals guiding lower-level ones. This provides consistent guidance and helps ensure that the work people do will fit together and create the desired outcome.

Vision, Goals, Objectives, and OKRs

I find that some people get confused by the terms *vision, goal,* and *objective.* Here is how I use them: A *vision* is a high-level, overarching goal that is typically ambitious and inspirational. Consequently, it cannot be measured.

A *goal* expresses an aim, something we want to achieve. Some goals are big and may never be fully realised, like a vision; others are SMART—specific, measurable, agreed upon, realistic, and timebound, like a sprint goal.

An *objective* is a goal that can be measured. You can therefore select metrics to determine progress towards the goal. If the goal is strategic in nature, like a user or business goal, then the metrics would be typically referred to as *key performance indicators or KPIs.*

OKRs (objectives and key results) are the measures used to determine if an objective has been met. If you currently employ OKRs to define and measure goals for your product, then that's great. But I would encourage you to review them to ensure that they are systematically linked and fulfil the criteria suggested earlier.

Be Goal-Led, Not Goal-Driven

Working towards goals feels natural to many people. You might even feel that without them, you lack direction and meaning. That's no coincidence: We are conditioned to achieve goals from an early age, at least in the West. We are encouraged to pass tests and get good grades, earn a good degree, get a good job, and the list goes on. While there is nothing wrong with setting goals and working towards them, we should be careful not to tie our self-worth to them.

Say you set yourself the goal to run ten kilometres in under fifty minutes. You train hard for it, but despite your best effort, you fail to accomplish your goal. How would you then feel? The answer will depend on how important the achievement is to you. If it is significant, then you may be miserable. You might even think of yourself as a failure and consequently suffer from low self-confidence. The same is true for product-related goals: If you are desperate to succeed, then failing to meet a goal will leave you at least feeling disappointed. But despite your best effort, it's not always possible to achieve success. Products die young, and failure is part and parcel of innovation. There is no guarantee that your product will meet its goals and become a success. The harder you try and the more you want success, the more difficult it will be for you to deal with failure.

But this does not mean that you should abandon goals. Instead, establish a healthy relationship with them. Don't cling to them but hold them lightly. While it's good to make the right effort to achieve your goals, put them into perspective, particularly when you start to get stressed or worried about achieving a goal. Ask yourself why meeting a goal is so important to you. And is it worth getting stressed, feeling anxious, becoming grumpy, and possibly losing sleep over it, for instance? What is the worst thing that could happen if you couldn't meet the goal?

If you miss a goal, recognise what happened and take responsibility. But don't be overly self-critical, and don't beat yourself up if you fail. This will only make you feel miserable, and it won't change anything for the better. Similarly, hold other people accountable for meeting agreed goals, and don't let them get away with ignoring goals they have agreed to. But be understanding when a goal is missed. Honour people's goodwill and be grateful for their effort.

Set Realistic Goals

I once worked for an organisation where an ambitious new product was developed. While everybody was enthusiastic at the outset, it quickly became apparent that launching the product on time and on budget was unrealistic. But instead of recognising this fact and changing plans, management decided to stick with the original goals and turned up the pressure. People were told to work overtime, and a bonus was promised for those who worked extra hard. Agile practices were suspended, and the development effort turned into a death march. The product finally shipped a year late with poor quality, after a number of people had left the company. Sadly, the product never became a success.

Setting unrealistic goals and pressuring people to achieve them is not uncommon in software development. While some say that people perform best under pressure, I regard this view as misguided. As human beings, we reach optimum performance when we are focused and relaxed. If you are stressed, tense, pressured, worried, or anxious, your ability to make the right decisions is significantly reduced; creativity and open-mindedness are severely affected. Additionally, people tend to worry most about how to get through the difficult experience; teamwork suffers; and velocity may be artificially increased by cutting corners and reducing quality, thereby making it harder to achieve future product goals.

I consequently recommend that you do your best to establish honest, realistic goals—goals that can be met—rather than "stretch" goals that are unrealistic from the outset and might negatively impact people's health. (I say more about stretch goals at the end of this section.) This requires two things: First, developing the right attitude towards goal achievement as previously described; and second, having the courage to say no to unrealistic expectations and unhealthy work practices. While there is a whole range of techniques and tools available to come up with sensible estimates and to set achievable goals, including story points, Planning Poker, and burndown charts, these will only help you if you are willing to face reality and do the right thing. It is all too easy to succumb to organisational pressure and wishful thinking, ignore the concerns of the development team, and insist on meeting aggressive goals. But this does not make them more realistic and achievable. Instead, it is likely to poison your relationship with the dev team and cause people to disengage. In the worst case, you will lose key members, and the targets will become even more unattainable.

If you think that this is all well in theory, but in practice you don't have a choice, then ask yourself what would happen if you declined agreeing to unrealistic goals while showing empathy with the requester and calmly explaining your reasons. If you feel that this would be completely unacceptable at your workplace, then reflect on why that is. Are you not sufficiently empowered? Or is the work culture unhealthy, as in the example described earlier? If so, can you bring about change? And if not, is it desirable to continue to work in such an environment? The decision I took in the story told earlier was to leave the company and set up my own business. But this step wasn't easy: Our oldest son was still very young at the time, and my wife was pregnant with our daughter.

Working with Stretch Goals

A stretch goal is a moon shot, a daring and ambitious goal that is extremely difficult to meet, according to Sitkin, Miller, and See (2017). The vision in figure 3 makes a great stretch goal: It is an ambitious goal that wants to inspire people. Remember, though, that the vision cannot be measured and may never be fully reached. All other goals discussed in this chapter should be realistic: You should be confident that the user, business, and product goals can be met, and so should the development team and stakeholders. Being overly ambitious and formulating these goals as stretch goals risks demotivating the development team and losing the trust of the stakeholders. Sprint goals, finally, must be realistic and achievable. Otherwise, the development team simply can't—and shouldn't—commit to them.

Choose Ethical Goals

Being the person in charge of the product can be tough: You have to ensure that your product generates value for the users *and* business. Otherwise, providing the product will become unsustainable: You burn through the company's money, but you don't generate any tangible business benefits. At the same time, many people are not willing to pay for digital products. How can you address this challenge?

One option some companies have chosen is to offer free digital products but to create a hook so that people keep coming back and continue to use the product. For example, I admit to being a lacklustre Facebook user who has disabled most of the product's notifications. Still, the company regularly sends me emails that say, "Roman, did you see [Facebook friend's name] comment on his status?" and "A lot has happened on Facebook since you last logged in. Here are some notifications you've missed from your friends." These messages want to entice me to use the product. Why? It increases engagement and helps sell advertisements and collect user data. Facebook is free. But developing and hosting the product obviously requires a significant investment. As Facebook does not want to introduce subscriptions or other forms of directly generating revenue at the time of writing, the company has to rely on selling ads and data—like many other companies that offer their digital products for free. The business model therefore gives rise to a product that can negatively impact the users' mental well-being.

But products should benefit people or, at least, not cause harm to anybody. This includes not intentionally encouraging addictive behaviour. We are all faced with the challenge to generate enough business value with our products. But users must come first. As I have mentioned before, you will find it difficult to generate sufficient business value in the long term if your product does not have a compelling value proposition and if it does not create real value for the users. What's more, while users are responsible for their actions, product people are responsible for the product's intended impact on the users. That is, if you offer a product that is intentionally designed to get people hooked, then your product is unethical in my mind.

Ethical Products

As product people, we have a responsibility for the impact our products create. If we can't guarantee that they will benefit people, then we should at least do everything we can to ensure that they are ethical—that they do not create any harm, neither to its users nor to the planet.

The former includes negatively impacting people's mental well-being, as discussed earlier. But it also means making ethical design and technology choices—for example, applying calm technology (Case 2015) and ethical product design principles (Rowe 2018)—as well as design for fairness when writing machine learning programs and avoiding algorithmic biases.

Additionally, consider the environmental impact your product has. Even though it may be digital, developing and hosting it still consumes energy. You should therefore consider choosing a carbon-neutral provider and reducing the amount of travelling you do, for instance, by using videoconferencing tools. And when you travel, choose transportation with low carbon emissions, like trains, whenever possible.

I would therefore encourage you to look for business goals and a business model that do not have a negative impact on the users. I firmly believe that people are willing to pay for a product when they regard it as truly valuable. Additionally, paying for digital products and content is becoming more acceptable. Take the change in online media that's happening at the time of writing: More and more news companies charge for all or at least some of their online content—for example, using subscription and pay-per-view models. Finally, ethical goals naturally attract people. It feels good to work on goals that benefit people and that have a positive impact on users' lives.

Give People Ownership

Whichever goals you use, secure strong support from the people who should follow them. It's great to have an inspirational vision; it's wonderful to have meaningful user and business goals; it's brilliant to have specific product and sprint goals in place. But these goals are not worth much if the development team and stakeholders don't buy into them. Without strong enough buy-in, people either won't follow them and will pursue their personal goals, or they will follow them half-heartedly, acting out of obligation but without a sense of real responsibly. Consequently, the individuals won't be committed to meeting the goals. Aligning people will therefore feel like herding cats—a virtually impossible task.

The best way to achieve strong support is to actively involve the people in the goal-setting process and to give them shared ownership of the goals, using the collaborative decision-making practices discussed in the chapter *Decision-Making and Negotiation*. While a collaborative approach might initially be more work for you, it will pay off in the long run. I know an Englishman who worked as a product person for several years in Sweden. Initially, the collaborative work culture he encountered tested his patience: Development team members and stakeholders wanted to be involved in most product decisions, something he was not used to. But over time, he learnt to appreciate the benefits of collaborative decision-making: Once a goal had been agreed, everybody would stick to it. People felt a shared sense of responsibility, and they help each other to reach the goal.

If, however, you feel that a collaborative approach is not feasible, then consider running individual meetings with the stakeholders and development team to discuss draft goals, incorporate people's feedback, and rework the goals so that everybody can support them.[38] Pay particular attention to the vision, user, and business goals. If these goals are not understood and accepted, then getting people to follow product and sprint goals will be challenging.

No matter which approach you choose, avoid the following mistakes: Neither pressure individuals to agree with you nor leave it up to others to decide the goals.[39] Additionally, don't make weak compromises to strike a deal or to please people; don't be afraid to push back and say no when it's appropriate. By the same token, keep an open mind, and appreciate people's ideas and concerns, even if you feel they are not helpful or appropriate. When you care about the individuals and empathise with them, people are more likely to support a goal, even if they don't fully agree with it. The practices discussed in the chapter *Decision-Making and Negotiation* will help you with collaboratively determining goals.

---

38   Note that the product person and the development team should agree on the sprint goal. To put it differently, the Scrum framework prevents product people from pushing sprint goals on to the dev team.

39   Unless delegation is appropriate; see the chapter *Decision-Making and Negotiation* for more information on delegating decisions.

CONVERSATIONS

It was impossible to get a conversation going. Everybody was talking too much.
Yogi Berra

Conversations are at the heart of what we do as product people: We talk to users, customers, development team members, and stakeholders; we capture ideas, plans, and requirements; we listen to feedback and concerns; and we read and write emails. Effective conversations not only exchange information between people but also create a shared understanding, build connections, and establish trust. This chapter helps you reflect on and improve your listening and speaking habits so that you become even better at understanding and guiding people.[40]

Listen Deeply

Listening is at the heart of every successful conversation. Without it, we just talk at each other, but we don't understand and connect with the other person. Unfortunately, listening is an undervalued skill: Often, we are taught only how to speak well but not how to listen effectively.

---

40   Please note that I focus on oral conversations using spoken language. But many of the recommendations offered are equally applicable to reading and writing.

In addition, we tend to think of listening as something passive. But listening takes on an active, engaging quality when it's practised well.

Why Listening Really Matters for Product People

Listening matters to us as product people for the following reasons: It helps you acquire new information, it increases people's support in product decisions, and it allows you to build and strengthen connections.

As you typically don't hold all the knowledge required to make the right product decisions, you will benefit from listening to ideas, thoughts, concerns, and feedback from other people—including users, customers, stakeholders, and development team members. This helps you to acquire the relevant knowledge and to develop the necessary insights.

Tips for Starting a Conversation

I find that we can be so focused on getting things done that we sometimes don't take the time to check in and find out how people are at the beginning of a conversation. But this can make it hard to understand the other person and say the right things, as the following example shows. I was recently in a meeting where one of the attendees hogged the conversations and went off on a tangent. Asking her to let others contribute and reminding her of the objective of the meeting didn't help much. This left me irritated and confused. I couldn't understand the behaviour of the individual, who I know as smart and kind. Only when I talked to her after the meeting did I discover the real reason for her behaviour: She was going through a difficult phase in her divorce and was affected by worries and low self-esteem. I wished afterwards that we had spent a few minutes at the beginning of the meeting to invite everyone to briefly say how they are doing. This would have allowed us to (re)connect and helped us understand each other, thereby increasing the chances of having a successful meeting.

I therefore recommend that you start a conversation with a brief check-in. For a one-on-one meeting, a couple of minutes are usually enough, and for a larger meeting with, say, ten members, five minutes should be sufficient. One way to do this is to ask everyone present to briefly answer the following two questions: *How am I feeling right now?* (for instance, "I am tired, irritated, or excited") and *Why am I feeling this way?* (for example, "I slept badly last night," "I just had a difficult meeting," or "I am really looking forward to working with you"). Ask everyone to attentively listen, and thank everybody for sharing at the end. Applied correctly, checking in helps people become aware of their own mental state and empathise with each other. It also builds trust: People share personal information and learn more about each other.

Additionally, as the person in charge of the product, you require the support of the development team and the stakeholders to create and provide a great product. Inviting the individuals to share their ideas and views and carefully listening to what they have to say gives people the opportunity to be heard. It allows them to influence and shape decisions, and it makes them feel appreciated and understood. This increases the likelihood that people will follow your lead, even if you can't take all their suggestions on board.

Last but not least, effective listening not only helps you receive what is being said but also allows you to tune into the speaker's emotions and empathise with the person. This creates an emotional bond, an understanding that goes beyond words. At the same time, it increases the trust and respect others have for you, as I describe in the chapter *Introduction*.

Covey's Listening Levels

While listening is key to an effective conversation, we don't always listen well. As Steve Covey observed, "Most people do not listen with the intent to understand; they listen with the intent to reply" (Covey 2013, 251). I find that's certainly true for myself: I sometimes formulate an answer in my head while the other person is still speaking. Covey calls this *selective listening*, which is one of five listening levels stated in table 1.

Table 1: *Covey's Listening Levels*

Listening Level	Description
Level 1	Ignore
Level 2	Pretend to listen
Level 3	Selective listening
Level 4	Attentive listening
Level 5	Empathic listening

Let's look at examples of the listening levels in table 1. While few people intentionally ignore what others are saying or pretend to listen, listening at this level is not uncommon. Imagine that a development team member pops by your desk and asks you a question about a user story she or he is working on. But as you are immersed in answering an urgent email, you either ignore the question or pretend to listen by nodding your head or saying, "OK, all right." If that's the case, you apply listening level one, *ignore*, or level two, *pretend*, respectively. Similarly, if you make the effort to stop working on the email and give your attention to the team member but find that you are quickly lost in your own thoughts—possibly wondering why you regularly get questions about user stories during a sprint and what you could do to improve the situation—you've stopped paying attention to what is being said. You consequently receive no or little information, and you might have to apologise and ask the individual to repeat what she or he said.

The third level, *selective listening*, means that at least some information is received. This is common when you listen with a specific goal in mind. Say you host a product roadmapping workshop where the attendees discuss changes to the plan. But rather than listening with an open mind, you have already predetermined how the roadmap should be changed and want the workshop participants to agree with your idea. As a consequence, you are likely to filter what is being said, primarily hear what supports your view (which is also referred to as *confirmation bias*), and therefore obtain selected pieces of information.

The fourth level is called *attentive listening*. As its name suggests, you listen attentively when you pay close attention to what is being said. This listening level requires effort and concentration, and it can sometimes feel like hard work, particularly when you don't like what you are hearing, when you are tempted to follow your own thoughts, or when you are tired. While attentive listening allows you to receive everything that's being said, your focus is on the information exchanged.

The fifth and deepest listening level is *empathic listening*, which is also referred to as *active*, *deep*, and *effective listening*. When listening with empathy, you not only receive what is being said but also connect and empathise with the speaker, without necessarily agreeing with the individual. This makes people feel understood and appreciated, and it builds and strengthens relationships. But it requires not only your full attention but also an open, non-judgemental mind and a warm, caring attitude: You have to listen with the intent to understand, not to critique, convince, persuade, or win. Empathic listening is comparatively easy when you communicate with someone you like and agree with. But when you find the person difficult or you strongly disagree with the individual, it can be challenging. The following guidelines will help you effectively listen to people, no matter how disagreeable and unlikeable you might find them.

Listening and Hearing Impairments

Not all of us are fortunate enough to have a fully functioning hearing faculty. Some product people live with hearing loss, which can range from difficulty in understanding the other person in a telephone conversation to deafness. If you have a hearing impairment, then you are likely to find that some of the techniques discussed in this section won't work for you. But that's all right: My intention is not so much to tell the reader to use specific methods. Instead, I want to encourage you to foster an attitude of openness, receptivity, and care. In this sense, you can deeply "listen" by attentively reading someone's email or a conversation transcript, for example, while cultivating an open, non-judgemental mind.[41]

Listen Inwardly

Listening comes in two flavours: Listening to another person and receiving what is being said, and listening to the reactions triggered in our minds, noticing the thoughts and emotions that come up. Listening inwardly helps you avoid replying in an unhelpful

---

41 Thanks to John Barratt for making me aware of the challenges product people with hearing impairments face.

way—saying something you will later regret or using harsh, hurtful words. Therefore, pay attention to the feelings and thoughts that arise while you are listening. What is your emotional response to what you are hearing? How are the words affecting you? Are you feeling glad, sad, or indifferent? Are you getting upset, worried, or angry? Do you feel the urge to defend yourself or interrupt the other person? And if so, why is that?

Additionally, be mindful of your general mood before you start a conversation. Your mental state influences how you perceive reality; it affects how you interpret what you hear and how you respond to it. For example, when I am tired, tense, stressed, or grumpy, everything I hear tends to have a negative connotation. But when I am happy, even bad news doesn't seem to be that terrible. Being aware of your state of mind helps you anticipate how you are likely to react, and it puts your experience into perspective. Heightening your awareness and practicing mindfulness, as discussed in the chapter *Self-Leadership*, will help you with listening inwardly, being aware of your general mood and how your mind responds to what it perceives.

If you find that you are getting distracted or overwhelmed by your reaction to what you are hearing, then pause the conversation (Sofer 2018, 245). You might say to the other person, for example, "I'm feeling a little overwhelmed right now. Can you give me a minute to reflect on what I've heard you say?" Alternatively, you might use body language to indicate that you are processing what you've heard—for example, take a deep, audible breath. If you need more time, consider taking a longer break and postponing the conversation. You might say, "I'm committed to figuring this out together, but I can't think clearly right now. Can we take a break and continue tomorrow?"

Give the Other Person Your Full Attention

Try to give your full and undivided attention to the other person, particularly when you are having an important conversation. This makes the person feel appreciated. What's more, "when individuals feel listened to, they tend to listen to themselves more carefully and to openly evaluate and clarify their own thoughts and feelings. In addition, they tend to become less defensive and oppositional and more willing to listen to other points of view," observes Voss (2016, 16). In practice, however, attentive listening can be hard: As product people, we have many different duties competing for our time and attention, and your mind might be full of other thoughts and ideas that make it hard to stay focused and receptive. If that's the case for you, then try the following three tips:

First, don't add too many meetings to your calendar. Giving someone your full attention is very challenging when you have to rush from one meeting to the next—it's likely to leave you feeling restless, tense, and tired. Therefore, schedule enough time for each conversation and plan in extra time beforehand and afterwards, particularly for important conversations—at least fifteen minutes as a rule of thumb. This gives you time to get ready for the meeting, and it allows you to process it afterwards, both intellectually and emotionally. Second, minimise any distractions and interruptions. Close your laptop or tablet, mute or switch off your phone, and use a meeting room, if appropriate. Third, turn your body towards the speaker, look directly but respectfully at the person, and establish eye contact—unless that's socially unacceptable, of course. This signals that you are paying attention and are interested in what the other person has to say, and it helps you take in the person's body language.

If you can't offer your undivided attention, then consider postponing the conversation: Listening to someone does not make sense if you are not fully present, as you won't be able to receive all the information, let alone build an emotional connection with the person. What's more, not paying attention sends a bad message to the individual: The person will think that she or he is not important enough to gain your full attention.

Pay Attention to the Person's Body Language

While words are undoubtedly important, human communication also involves body language, including voice pitch and volume, facial expressions, eye movement, gestures, and stance. If somebody tells you, for example, that she or he fully supports your product roadmap but rolls the eyes or pulls a face, you know that the individual is not being sincere. Equally, if the person has a red face and speaks loudly while providing feedback, you can tell that she or he is upset, no matter how carefully the person minces her or his words.

What's more, the nonverbal information helps you understand the speaker's intention. In the first example, the individual might want to make a joke and be jovial—or criticise and belittle the plan. In the second example, the person's body language may express strong disagreement or discontentment.

Therefore, pay close but respectful attention to the other person's body language and look out for inconsistencies, expressions that don't match the words. Additionally, prefer face-to-face meetings over email and telephone conversations, particularly for important conversations—be it in person or via videoconferences. As the "Manifesto for Agile Software Development" puts it, "The most efficient and effective method of conveying information…is face-to-face conversation" (Beck et al. 2001).

Listen with an Open Mind

To maximise the chances of connecting with the other person and learning something new, take a sincere interest in the individual and what she or he has to say. Make a conscious effort to listen with an open mind, and be respectfully curious. The following three techniques will help you cultivate an open mind: First, be mindful of how receptive you are during a conversation and notice when you are closing off. Your body is likely to provide helpful clues. I often get tense in my face, for example, when I am no longer open-minded. If you find yourself evaluating or judging what the other person is saying, then try to relax and cultivate self-compassion: We often habitually analyse and judge without being fully aware of it.

Second, develop a warm-hearted attitude towards the other person. Start by reflecting on the image you hold of the individual. What qualities do you associate with the person, and how do you relate to the individual? If you find the person difficult or unlikeable, bring to mind the person's positive traits. Think of the good things the person has said or done. This helps you be less critical and judgemental while listening to someone, and it therefore increases your ability to be receptive and connect with the other person.

Third, reflect on your own ideas and views and why they are important to you. I find that I can suffer from expert syndrome—the more I know about a subject, the less open I tend to be to other people's views. If this happens to you, then try to take your ideas less personally. After all, none of us was born with the ideas and beliefs we carry with us. We've acquired the vast majority of them from other people, sometimes without being fully aware of them. Additionally, try to be humble and grateful for other people's perspectives, even if you disagree with them or regard them as inappropriate. We can still learn something from an ill-conceived idea, even if it's only how easy it is to fall prey to our biases.

A Simple Listening Exercise

If you want to strengthen your ability to listen attentively and open-mindedly, then try the following exercise: Think of the type of music you like to listen to. Then consider the music you dislike. For example, you might enjoy listening to baroque music but dislike punk, or you might be into progressive rock or metal but despise jazz. Next, choose a piece of music from the genre you dislike and carefully listen to it. Observe what thoughts and feelings arise while you are listening and how they affect you. Acknowledge any negative emotions that might come up, but try to stay with the music and be receptive and curious. Despite the fact that you might not enjoy the experience and still dislike the music, is there something you can learn? You might be fascinated by the virtuosity of the jazz players, for example, or you might be impressed by the raw power of a metal song. If you complete the exercise, you should have improved your listening skills, and you might have discovered that there is more interesting music out there than you had assumed.

Listen for Facts, Feelings, and Needs

Whenever you are in a conversation, don't listen only to the facts; go deeper and also listen for feelings and needs (see Cohen, Partnow, and Green 2017, Loc 435–51).

Facts describe *what* is being said. They are the pieces of information people exchange—for instance, ideas about how to evolve a product's value proposition in order to keep it successful. To ensure that you have correctly understood what someone said, consider asking clarifying questions or summarising what you have heard. You may want to say, for example, "Can you please tell me more about…," or "I heard you say…" Additionally, use open questions, which typically start with *why*, *how*, or *what*, in order to find out more and encourage the other person to continue.

Asking Questions

Asking questions not only helps you learn more about the thoughts and feelings of the other person but also makes people feel appreciated and builds strong relationships: They signal that you are listening and want to know more. Additionally, questions encourage people to come up with answers themselves. This leverages their creativity and generates buy-in to a solution or course of action.[42]

But not all questions are appropriate in a given context. Open questions encourage people to provide more information—for example, "What do you think of the latest strategy update?" or "How can we meet the product roadmap goals?" Closed questions—which can be answered by a *yes* or *no*—are useful for concluding a discussion or making a decision—for example, "Do you agree that this is the right course of action?"—as well as for testing your understanding—for instance, "It is correct that you cannot do any architecture refactoring work in the upcoming sprint?"

But as mentioned earlier, you should apply closed questions carefully. They carry the risk of bias and manipulation, as you limit the answers available to your conversation partner. Similarly, switching questions, which change the topic, can be great to move on the conversation. You might say, for example, "I understand you are concerned about enhancing the user experience. But what do you think about the prospect of addressing a new market segment and extending the functionality?" Switching questions can, however, also prevent the other person from being fully heard and understood. This can leave the individual feeling hurt and rejected.

Additionally, some questions should be avoided altogether, such as leading questions, which encourage the answer you want to hear. A question like "We have all agreed that the current strategy is the right way forward, haven't we?" strongly encourages people to support your view and not to challenge the plan.

---

42   This method is often applied in coaching, as it leverages people's creativity and knowledge and encourages them to take ownership. It is also referred to as the *Socratic method*: Socrates aimed to help his students discover answers by asking them questions.

Feelings are the emotions that are present when we express our thoughts, such as excitement, enthusiasm, frustration, or sadness. They tell us *how* a person is while speaking. The speaker's choice of words, pitch, volume, and facial expressions, including eye movements, gestures, and other body language elements, often reveal her or his feelings. At one time I was working with an organisation where the head of development sometimes attended the Daily Scrums. While he never said a word, his body language clearly showed when he was unhappy with what he heard: He would shift his weight from one foot to the other, roll his eyes, and occasionally even shake his head.

Needs, finally, are the underlying motives we have when we speak. They refer to our intentions and goals and describe *why* we say what we are saying. Imagine that you are in a strategy workshop where you discuss options to keep the product successful. Mark, the salesperson, is opposed to changing the product's value proposition. He uses the latest sales figures to argue that the current proposition is working very well—even though other key performance indicators (KPIs) clearly show that the product's attractiveness is decreasing. What might be the motivation behind Mark's argument? The desire to meet his sales targets and claim a bonus? A selfless motivation to offer the best possible product? Is it a combination of both? How can you tell?

A great way to discover the needs behind people's words is to ask *why* questions. In the previous scenario, you could ask Mark why he is concerned about amending the value proposition, for instance. Are there any negative consequences he anticipates? As this example shows, it is not always straightforward to understand people's needs during a conversation. But I find that this is crucial, particularly for high-impact decisions: If you ignore people's needs, then they are unlikely to support the decision. They might pay lip service to it, but they are unlikely to follow it through.

Therefore, don't exclusively focus on the words you hear, but pay attention to the individual's body language to understand the person's feelings. These can help you unearth the underlying needs, the reasons why the speaker says what she or he does. Listening for needs therefore provides you with deeper insights. It allows you to understand people's motives, wishes, and concerns.

Listen with Patience

How often does someone listen to you attentively without making you feel rushed or interrupting you? And how often do you listen to others in the same way? Giving people the time to finish what they have to say makes them feel valued, it builds trust and rapport, and it can reveal new pieces of information. But patiently listening is sometimes hard, particularly when you are busy or stressed. Interrupting the other person, however, is not only impolite but also can make the person feel insecure, rejected, hurt, or even angry. As a consequence, the individual will be less receptive to what you have to say or even reject your response in an attempt to retaliate—no matter how factually correct your answer is. Therefore, allow the other person to finish before you answer, even if that's challenging. The following four techniques can help you with this:

First, take three deep breaths or count to ten before you answer. This gives the individual enough time to continue and to finish her or his story without feeling rushed, and it allows you to let what you have heard sink in before you answer. Second, be mindful of your body language. If you get fidgety and, for example, start moving around on your seat, drumming your fingers, or shaking your legs, then you express impatience and restlessness. Third, learn to be comfortable with silence. I find that many people, including myself, are uneasy with tolerating silence in conversations: I can be so busy and restless that I want to progress and quickly finish the conversation without being fully aware of it; I might be enjoying it so much that I don't want it to stop; or I feel I have to say something to prevent the other person from thinking that I am lost for words. But silence is often necessary to encourage the other person to continue to talk and to share something that might be uncomfortable or difficult. Fourth, consider timeboxing people's contributions in meetings to avoid the risk of long monologues. For instance, everyone has two minutes to share their perspectives. When the time is up, the person must stop talking, and it's the next individual's turn.

Don't forget, however, to take care of yourself. If you are patiently listening but find it increasingly hard to bear what you are hearing, then consider switching the topic or ending the conversation. Some conversations can turn poisonous, in which case it is best to stop and continue at a later point in time. But leave a difficult conversation without making things worse, without accusing and blaming the other person. This will help you restart the conversation and repair the relationship.

Speak Effectively

Words can inspire, comfort, and connect. But they can also hurt and divide. To help maximise the chances that your message is received and at the same time strengthen your bond with the listeners, I recommend a Buddhist teaching called *Right Speech*.[43] The teaching offers the following five guidelines: Speak with the right intention; say only what you believe is true; only speak if it's beneficial for the people listening; don't use harsh or harmful words; and make sure you speak at the right time and place, and I would add, using the right channel.

Well Intended

To maximise the chances that people will take in what you have to say, speak with care and warm-heartedness. In practice, however, I

---

43 In Buddhism, speech holds an important place. Right Speech (*samma vaca*) is the third practice of the Noble Eightfold Path. It is described in two ways in Buddhist scriptures: The Magga-vibhanga Sutta (SN 45.8) characterises it as "abstaining from lying, from divisive speech, from abusive speech, and from idle chatter." The Anguttara Nikaya Sutta (AN 5.198) states, "It is spoken at the right time. It is spoken in truth. It is spoken affectionately. It is spoken beneficially. It is spoken with a mind of good-will" (Thanissaro 2013). Note that *samma* can also be translated as "perfected" and "completed." You can therefore think of Right Speech as speech that has been perfected.

find that my intentions vary. They can be skilful, like sharing a piece of information someone needs and making an individual feel at ease. But they can also be self-centred, such as wanting to be perceived as smart or funny and having a go at somebody to put the individual in her or his place. Sometimes intentions are mixed with altruistic and selfish motives intermingled. For example, you might want to help someone understand why you had to remove a feature from the current release, but you might also want to avoid having people think you are bad at planning. If that's the case, determine your primary intention, the main reason for speaking.

Should You Persuade People?

Persuasion means wording a request so that the other person complies with it, usually by triggering an automatic, subconscious reaction (Cialdini 2009). For example, in order to make a stakeholder agree to a maintenance release, you might say, "As you understand the importance of good product quality and have supported maintenance work in the past, you will surely agree that a maintenance release is now required to remove bigger issues and to future-proof the product." This example uses consistency as a persuasion technique—people usually like to be consistent with their past actions. Another way to persuade the individual would be to say, "The head of sales and the head of marketing also support a maintenance release to future-proof the product." In this case, you would use social pressure to make the other person agree with you.

Persuasion is often considered a standard approach to achieve buy-in and create alignment. But is it right to persuade others? Is it OK to get people to do what you consider right? I would encourage you to carefully look at your intentions. Consider why you want somebody to do something and what the consequences are when you persuade someone. Will the individual still support your request when she or he has had the opportunity to reflect on what happened, or will the person feel cheated or even manipulated? Instead of trying to persuade someone and make the person comply to a request, try to understand the individual's needs and involve the person in the decision-making process, as I discuss in more detail in the chapter *Decision-Making and Negotiation*.

While your intentions might not always be wholesome, becoming aware of them helps you avoid saying something that you may later regret, that might damage the relationship and destroy the trust of the other person. If you find that your intention is not right, if your speech is self-centred or affected by unskilful emotions like anger, ill will, anxiety, and fear, then you should consider pausing and remaining silent, at least for a few seconds. Don't feel pressured to say something, and resist the impulse to immediately offer a proper answer, particularly if you are affected by difficult emotions like confusion, anger, or worries. Instead, say, for instance, "I am sorry, but I am feeling confused/upset/angry right now. I need a minute to digest what I heard you say." This tells the other person how her or his words have affected you, and it buys you time to reflect on your emotions and intentions and decide how to respond. You can take this further and habitually insert small pauses into your conversations. This will create moments of choice for you and reduce the likelihood that you will speak on autopilot, only realising what you are saying once the words have been verbalised.[44]

True

The second guideline is to say only what you consider to be true and not to lie intentionally.

At first glance, this advice seems rather trivial—aren't we taught from an early age that lying is bad, that it destroys trust and respect? But on reflection, it is sometimes hard to tell what is true. Let's say, for example, that the sign-up rate of your product has been declining for several months, but revenue is still strong. What, then, is your conclusion, your version of the truth? Is it that everything is fine and the drop is just a temporary blip? Or do you believe that trouble is just around the corner? As this simple example shows, what we regard as true is—at least to a certain extent—subjective. It depends on our interpretation of the facts, which is influenced by our state of mind, our biases, and our preconceived ideas. Consequently, what you regard as true might not be seen as true by the development team or stakeholders.

---

44 I've adopted the term *moment of choice* from Marc Abraham. Thanks for suggesting it!

But telling the truth involves more than factual accuracy. Let's continue the previous example and say that your boss asks you how your product is doing. You answer her by saying, "Not bad." Are you then being truthful? It seems to me that this answer is neither the truth nor a proper lie—it's somewhere in between. A more appropriate reply might be, "I am not sure; the data I have are inconclusive: Revenue is looking good, but the sign-up rate is dropping." I find, however, that we often bend the truth a little bit to avoid a difficult conversation or disappointing someone or to protect our interests.

I once had a boss who looked at me sternly whenever I said something he disapproved of, so I avoided telling him any "bad" news. Instead, I sugar-coated it and made it sound as nice as possible. While my reaction might be understandable, it would have been better to be courageous and to say things how they were. If we start bending the truth, making something or someone look better or worse, or exaggerating or minimising a fact, we are on a slippery slope. When people find out, will they continue to respect and trust us? And in the story with my boss, did I not indirectly support his inappropriate behaviour by bending the truth?

True speech is therefore not over- or understated, taken out of context, or blown up or blown out of proportion. It doesn't encourage people to draw the wrong conclusions, like a stakeholder believing you will fulfil her or his feature request when you say, "There is a chance that we are able to do it in the next release," but you know you won't be able to do it. Finally, true speech means not using any vanity metrics that make your product look good but that don't help people understand how it's doing.

Beneficial

Once you have established the right intention and have ensured that you speak the truth, check that the message is actually helpful for the listener, that the individual will benefit from hearing what you want to say. This, however, does not mean that the listener must like or agree with your message.

I remember once being asked for advice. The individual wanted to know what she should do so that her management would allow her to own the product roadmap. When I suggested that she might want to strengthen her roadmapping skills, she wasn't too impressed. It seemed to me that she'd hoped for an answer that required her management to change but not herself. While the individual didn't like my advice, I still believe that it was beneficial for her.

As this example shows, speaking beneficially can be challenging when different ideas and interests are present or when a problem has to be addressed. Say your Scrum Master, Sue, has done a great job teaching the development team and you how to apply Scrum and to progress your product. But recently she has been so busy coaching another team that she hasn't been able to offer much support to your team. Consequently, the development process has started to show cracks, such as team members coming late to Daily Scrums and tasks not being updated regularly. As you are concerned about the situation, you've set up a meeting with Sue. You start the conversation by saying, "Thank you for meeting with me, Sue. I am concerned about my team. People no longer follow all the Scrum guidelines. The Daily Scrum this morning was pretty chaotic again. I am worried that this will impact the team performance and our ability to get the next release out as planned. I really want you to be around more and help the team." This may sound like a reasonable request: It's clear and specific. But imagine how it might affect Sue. She surely must be aware that she can't support your team enough; she might even feel guilty and frustrated. This may cause her to interpret your request as an attack, thinking that you are blaming her for the development team's issues, even though that was not your intention. Instead of sharing perspectives and finding a way forward, you may end up experiencing conflict and friction. How can you avoid such an undesirable outcome?

Positive First

Before you say something critical or negative, first share a positive observation.[45] Applying this technique to the previous example, you would initially thank Sue for her hard work and praise her for the great job she's done for your team before you address the problem. The positive feedback, however, must be genuine and not empty flattery. Otherwise, the listener is likely to sense that you are not telling the truth and therefore will distrust you.

Flipping and Framing

Another way to help people receive a difficult message is using *flipping* and *framing*, two appreciative inquiry techniques. Instead of saying, for example, "You don't spend enough time with the team," you flip the message and communicate the positive opposite together with the desired outcome. Consequently, you might say, "It would be great if you could spend more time with the team again so that you can help the members apply Scrum effectively." Stavros and Torres (2018, Loc 816–19) suggest three steps to change a negative piece of information into a desired benefit:

- Name it: What is the problem?
- Flip it: What is the positive opposite?
- Frame it: What is the desired outcome of the positive opposite?

When used properly, the *positive first, flipping,* and *framing* strategies help you avoid being overly critical and dwelling on the negatives. Now, I am not suggesting that you should sugar-coat everything you say or even ignore problems. But I know from my own experience that if I focus too much on what is wrong, I end up feeling miserable, and so do the people I talk to. Therefore, be frank and honest, but choose words that have a positive impact on the individual and that

---

45 I learnt this technique many years ago when working with design patterns at Siemens Corporate Technology, thanks to Frank Buschmann and Michael Stahl. But I don't know who first suggested it.

help the person to take in your message—rather than causing the person to close off or attack you.

Separate Problem and Person

Whenever addressing a problem, make sure that you separate the issue from the person. Say you believe that Sue has a tendency to overcommit and take on too much work. You might then be tempted to tell her, "I wish you would stop taking on too much work." But would this approach be helpful? Would it be beneficial to tell Sue what you believe is wrong with her? Chances are that it would cause Sue to be defensive and justify her behaviour or that she would interpret it as unfair criticism and launch a counterattack, possibly accusing you of some wrongdoing. But it is unlikely to help resolve the issue or strengthen her trust in you.

Therefore, separate the problem from the individual. Instead of telling Sue what she does wrong, ask her what she thinks, how she feels, and what she would like to do. We usually don't encourage others to change by telling them what is wrong with them but by carefully listening to them and empathising with them. You might ask Sue, for instance, why she thinks that she is stretched at present and what she intends to do to improve things. This way, Sue will hopefully discover for herself that she should take on less work in the future and be more realistic about how many teams she can support concurrently.

Modulate Your Pace

I find that it's easy to get carried away, particularly in a group conversation, to speak too fast and maybe talk too much, and in the worst case, hog the conversation and make the other people feel uneasy. Additionally, speaking at a high pace can make it difficult for the listeners to take in what you are saying. People might be overwhelmed by the amount of information you share. To prevent these issues, make an effort to modulate your pace and to slow down. Consider using short, intentional pauses that allow you to relax, breathe, and be present, that help the listeners process what they've heard, and that give them the opportunity to contribute.

Kind

Kind speech means using words that help, not harm, people. It means treating your listeners with respect—no matter what they may have said or done. My experience suggests that practicing kind speech is easy when we talk to someone we like or at least don't find difficult. But when a difficult person is involved, someone we dislike or whose attitude or behaviour we find challenging, then speaking with kindness can be hard, as the following example shows.

Responding to Difficult Messages

Say that Julie, a senior stakeholder, keeps challenging the goals on the product roadmap despite having been involved in the decision-making process. To make things worse, you find Julie an unlikeable person, someone who has strong views and believes she is right. Let's assume that you are talking to her in private, asking her why she keeps challenging the plan. If she then tells you, "It's because you disregard other people's ideas and pressure everyone to agree with your views," your initial reaction might be anger. Consequently, you might snap back at her and say, "That's not true. We had an open discussion in which you participated, but you've chosen to disregard the group decision. You are arrogant to think that you know better and don't have to follow a group decision." While such a reaction is understandable, it would hardly be helpful: Labelling Julie as arrogant would probably cause her to disengage from the conversation or to launch a counterattack. The former would end the discussion; the latter could lead to a bruising verbal fight. Either way, the issue would not get resolved. But the trust and respect between Julie and you would be damaged and the connection weakened.

How could you speak kindly to Julie, without ignoring or glossing over her behaviour? First, you could deliberately pause, a technique I mentioned earlier. This would allow you to become aware of your feelings and to regain your composure. Next, you might say, for example, "I am sorry to hear that you feel this way, Julie. I understand that you are unhappy with the product roadmap, but I don't share your perspective. As far as I can remember, you were actively involved in the roadmap decisions, and everyone else is happy with the goals. Can you please tell me why you think that I've ignored your ideas and why you feel pressured to agree with me?" This would allow you to express your perspective and at the same time encourage Julie to share more information.[46] Kind speech is therefore not about only saying nice things, always being cheerful and smiley, and ignoring difficulties and problems or sugar-coating them. It is about caring about the effect your words are likely to have on the other person and avoiding harsh, offensive, dismissive, judgemental, cynical, nasty, and divisive speech.

In order to speak kindly, try the following three tips: First, keep your speech free from anger or other unwholesome emotions—even when you feel unfairly treated, offended, or hurt. Responding to anger with anger will only worsen things. Consider not answering immediately but pausing for a few seconds to become aware of your feelings and to decide how to best respond. Second, be grateful for the other person's time and interest, even if you disagree with the individual or don't find the message very helpful. In the previous example, you might want to appreciate the fact that Julie is at least willing to engage in a conversation with you and share her perspective. Third, apply kind speech not only to the people who are present but also to those who are not. Avoid talking badly about others, and refrain from malicious gossip, divisive speech, and unkind comparisons.

What's Wrong with Some Gossip?

Gossip is common in many workplaces, and I have gossiped myself on more than one occasion. Isn't gossip helpful? Doesn't it feel good to slag off a difficult boss while having coffee with some colleagues? It seems to get rid of irritation and anger, and it builds rapport. At times, you might even feel obliged to join in to show that you are part of the group. But unkind gossip has a dark side: It reinforces negative thoughts and emotions rather than cleansing them. What's more, a group that is built on the belief that its members are in some way better than others is unlikely to be wholesome. To achieve great things, focus on what unites people, not on what sets them apart.

---

46 See the chapter *Conflict* for more help on dealing with difficult people and conflict.

Saying No in the Right Way

Let's say that John, the sales rep, and you are having lunch together. After some initial chit-chat, John mentions the upcoming release and strongly suggests adding a new feature. But you know that there is no chance that you can take on the feature without moving the date. What's more, it doesn't help meet the goal of the release, which makes you think that John's request might be partly motivated by the desire to meet his sales targets. Consequently, you may be tempted to say, "Sorry, John. But there is no way I can add the feature. It doesn't support the product goal of the current release, and we are struggling to cope with the amount of work as it is." This may seem like a reasonable answer. It explains why you have to decline his request. But is it kind?

Mind Your Own Body Language

While the words you choose matter, don't forget to be mindful of your body language, including your voice pitch and volume, facial expressions, eye movement, gestures, and stance. Ensure that you respectfully look at the other person and make eye contact while talking, assuming that's socially acceptable. This shows the other person that you are present and care about the impact of your words. Additionally, it allows you to see how the listener is responding to your message. Is the individual looking pleased, surprised, bored, tired, annoyed, angry, or indifferent? And what does this tell you about your speech?

Saying no is part and parcel of a product person's job: It is impossible to please everyone. If, however, the person whose idea or request has been declined does not feel understood or even feels rejected, then it will be hard for the individual to accept no as an answer; the person might be disappointed or angry. I therefore recommend that you try to say no in a firm but caring way. Empathise with the individual and be grateful for the suggestion or request, even if you disagree with it. This will make it easier for the person to accept the message. In the previous example, you might reply to John, "Thank you for suggesting the feature, John. It sounds like it's important to you. I am really sorry; I am struggling to see how we can accommodate it right now. But can you please tell me why you want to see it added?" This way you express your gratitude for John's effort; you show that you understand that the request is important to him; you explain why you can't say yes at present; and you encourage John to say more about his reason for requesting the feature, which tells John that you value his input and want to continue the conversation.

Well Timed

Finally, make sure that you speak at the right time, in the right place, and through the right channel to maximise the chances that your message will be understood. Ask yourself if the other person is able to take in the information. When someone is tired or preoccupied with other thoughts, it is usually better to postpone the conversation, particularly if it is an important one. If you are at the end of a workshop where you've spent the last two hours brainstorming and discussing ideas for improving the product performance, then it would probably be unwise to bring up a new topic without first having a proper break. Chances are that the topic would not receive the necessary attention, and people might leave the meeting feeling tired and grumpy.

Similarly, consider the best way to communicate your message. While using email and other text-based messages can be more convenient and comfortable than speaking to someone in person, particularly important and difficult conversations benefit from talking face to face, where people are either in the same room or participate in a video call. This allows you to see the body language of the other person and to better understand how she or he responds to what you are saying. This makes it easier to understand and empathise with the individual, choose the right words, and communicate effectively.

A Summary of Selected Conversation Techniques

This section brings together selected listening and speaking techniques, most of which I have used in examples throughout this chapter. The techniques listed will help you reflect on and improve how you engage in conversations. When applying the techniques listed in table 2, ensure that you have the right intention. Use them to understand and connect with people, not to make someone agree to or do something. This is particularly true for techniques like *drawing out* and *mirroring*, which can trick people into a false sense of trust if they are not applied with honesty and integrity. As with other techniques, you will become better at applying them over time by putting them in practice and investigating how you can apply them even more effectively.

Table 2: *Selected Conversation Techniques*[47]

Technique	Description
Paraphrase	In your own words, say what you think the speaker has said and ask the individual if you have paraphrased it correctly.
Summarise	Sum up what the other person says to check that you heard correctly and to give the speaker the opportunity to reflect on what she or he said.
Clarify	Asking clarifying questions ensures that you have correctly understood what was said, and it encourages people to provide more information. You might say, for instance, "Can you please give me an example of what you mean?"
Mirror	Repeat the exact same words in a warm and accepting voice, no matter if you agree with what was said or not.
Draw out the other person	Paraphrase the speaker's statement, then ask open-ended, non-directive questions to encourage the individual to share more information. You might say, "Can you please tell me more about this?"

---

47   The conversation techniques are based on based on Kaner et al. (2014), Sofer (2018), and Stavros and Torres (2018).

Acknowledge the feelings of the other person	People often communicate their feelings indirectly by using nonverbal means, like tone and facial expression. By identifying and naming a feeling, you show that you understand the other person. You might say, for example, "You look concerned."
Encourage	Encourage the speaker to continue. This demonstrates that you are paying attention and are interested in what the individual has to say. Consider maintaining eye contact, nodding your head, or saying, "Hmm" or "OK."
Pause	Intentionally stay silent for a moment. For example, take three deep breaths or count to ten. This allows you to reflect on what you have heard and to become aware of how you are feeling before you answer. You might want to say, "This sounds important. Can we pause here for a moment so that I can let it sink in?"
Postpone the conversation	Postpone continuing the conversation if you feel that no meaningful progress can be made right now, possibly due to the presence of strong, difficult emotions. You might say, "I'd really like to continue our conversation. As I'm feeling a little overwhelmed, I don't think I'll be able to listen well. Could we take a break and continue tomorrow?"
Chunk	Share one piece of information at a time. Speak in short, succinct chunks by breaking up a complex topic into smaller parts. This makes it easier for others to understand you.
Positive first	Before you say something critical or negative, first share a positive observation. Make sure that the positive feedback is genuine, and avoid empty flattery.
Flipping	Instead of discussing what's wrong, communicate the positive opposite, the outcome you'd like to achieve. For example, instead of saying, "You always come late to the product backlog refinement meeting," say, "It would be great if you could be on time for the refinement meeting." This focuses the conversation on what you'd like to achieve and avoids dwelling on the negatives.
Track	Keep track of the topics the conversation touches upon to avoid going off on tangents. This is particularly valuable in group conversations.
Redirect	Acknowledge what the other person has said and state your desire to return to a previous topic or to move on to a new one. This allows you to get the conversation back on track, in case of going off on a tangent, and it avoids one issue becoming too dominant.

CONFLICT

The ultimate measure of a man is not where he stands in moments of comfort and convenience, but where he stands at times of challenge and controversy.
Martin Luther King, Jr.

Conflict happens when one or more people are in disagreement and experience a clash of interests. It is perfectly normal, and it routinely occurs at work when people with different perspectives, needs, and goals engage. In fact, effective collaboration is hard to achieve if we haven't learnt to constructively deal with conflict.[48] And therein lies the challenge: Most of the conflicts I have witnessed at work were not handled skilfully; some were suppressed and ignored, and most were never properly resolved, leaving behind a trail of bad feelings and mistrust. But the problem is not the fact that we experience conflict; it is how we deal with it. If we learn to constructively address it, conflict will become a source of creativity and innovation for our products.[49]

---

48 Tuckman (1965), for example, suggests that a group has to go through a storming phase characterised by conflict before the individuals can gel into a productive, performing team; Lencioni (2002) describes how a lack of constructive conflict can hold a team back and lead to artificial but unproductive harmony.

49 Please note that I assume that the conflict can be resolved by the people involved, unlike severe transgressions such as violence, sexual harassment, and discrimination. If you are in doubt, do involve your line manager and human resources.

Avoid These Common Pitfalls

While conflict is a firm part of our human experience, we frequently resort to ineffective conflict resolution strategies and repeat the same mistakes, often without being aware of them. To help you reflect on how you deal with disagreements, I discuss five common pitfalls next. These are *win-lose*—believing that there must be a winner and a loser; *truth assumption*—assuming that the other person is wrong; *problem-solving mode*—seeing the disagreement as a primarily intellectual issue; *blame game*—assigning fault to the other person; and *artificial harmony*—ignoring conflict.

Win-Lose

One of the reasons why the term *conflict* has a negative connotation for many people is our experience of how disagreements play out: More often than not, one person wins and the other loses. For example, you tell your boss that you need another experienced UX designer to meet the goals on your product roadmap, but she disagrees and tells you to get on with it: Your boss wins, and you lose. Or the development team asks you to reprioritise the product backlog to account for a technical risk, but you disagree and ask the team to focus on the sprint goal: You win, and the team loses. This experience gives rise to four common but unhelpful conflict strategies: *competitive confrontation, passive aggression, conflict avoidance, and passivity* (Sofer 2018). The first two approaches are usually chosen to win; the latter two help you minimise your losses. Let's take a closer look at these four strategies.

Competitive Confrontation

Employing competitive confrontation means being forceful and pushing for what you want. This approach is often characterised by a strong focus on your own needs and by some form of aggressive behaviour. Competitive confrontation can manifest itself in raising the voice, blaming, judging, demanding, or even trying to coerce and manipulate others. Common underlying assumptions include the following (Sofer 2018, 67):

- If I don't stand up and fight, I'll lose out and my interests will be sidelined.
- Any empathy I show will be seen as vulnerability and used against me.
- I'm right; they're wrong (an assumption I discuss in more detail in the next section).

Passive Aggression

This strategy is an indirect form of confrontation: While pretending that all is well, you engage by expressing displeasure or resentment. For example, if you had an argument with the Scrum Master and now ignore the individual or refuse to speak to her or him, you are showing signs of passive-aggressive behaviour. Beliefs that give rise to this behaviour include the following (Sofer 2018, 69):

- I am being treated unfairly.
- No one really cares about what I want.
- Speaking up won't make a difference; it could make things worse.

Conflict Avoidance

As its name suggests, this behaviour aims to stay clear of conflict, often to preserve harmony and maintain relationships—at least temporarily. It is based on one or more of the following beliefs (Sofer 2018, 55):

- Conflict is dangerous.
- More harm will be caused if I try to address the issue than if I let it be.
- If I don't deal with it, it will go away or resolve itself.

Passivity

Last but not least, passivity is the opposite of competitive confrontation: You give up what you want and agree to the other person's requests or demands, thereby trying to appease the individual. Passivity is built on the following assumptions (Sofer 2018, 68):

- If I go along with this, everything will be fine.
- If I give others what they want, they'll like me.
- I've done something wrong; it's my fault.

Beyond Win-Lose

None of these four strategies results in sustainable positive outcomes. You might be able to get what you want or maintain harmony for a short while, for example, but the issue is likely to reappear sooner or later. Worse, all four strategies damage relationships and lead to a loss of trust, and they have a negative impact on your well-being—they are likely to give rise to resentment, worries, or anxiety. That's true for being confrontational and aggressive as well as for deprioritising or suppressing your needs.

Peace, Love, and Happiness

As human beings, we share the desire for harmony and peace, for living and working together in concord and happiness. But this does not mean that there can't or shouldn't be any conflicts. Instead, harmony and peace are established when we have learnt to constructively resolve conflict and have become more accepting of other people's perspectives and needs.

To skilfully deal with conflict, we must change our attitude: We should no longer see conflict as something that produces winners and losers but as an opportunity to connect, learn, and generate mutual gains. This is possible if we are willing to cultivate an open mind, attentively listen to the other person without being completely caught up in our ideas and emotions, and empathise with the individual. Of course, there is no guarantee that the individual will change her or his mind. But it is the best option we have to encourage change in the other person; see the behavioural change stairway model discussed in the chapter *Introduction*.

Truth Assumption

In theory, disagreeing with someone should be no big deal. After all, there are simply different opinions and perspectives present. So why do we sometimes get so wound up about another person's view? The cause is neatly expressed by the phrase, "I am right." Three things are at work here: First, we commonly assume that our perception of reality and perspective is correct. Consequently, the other person must be wrong—without being aware of this or questioning it (Stone, Patton, and Heen 2010).[50] Second, we are often attached to our ideas, opinions, and products, sometimes to the extent that we identify ourselves with them. When this happens, we are in danger of regarding disagreement as a personal criticism or an attack, even if this was not the other person's intention. Third, we may find it hard to admit that we are wrong, as we are driven by the desire to be right, to achieve and win.

Diverging Perceptions of Reality

We all see the world in slightly different ways: Our past experiences, knowledge, values, beliefs, and states of mind give rise to different interpretations of the same data, and our thinking is shaped by the ideas and beliefs we have, many of which we may not be aware of. As mentioned before, a difference of opinions is no problem at all unless we assume that our perception of reality, our interpretation of the data, is the only valid one. But as Mahatma Gandhi famously said, everybody holds a piece of the truth, and when it comes to making product decisions, you usually benefit from taking into account

---

50 I have borrowed *truth assumption*, *intention invention*, and *blame frame* from Stone, Patton, and Heen (2010), who describe them as common mistakes in difficult, conflict-rich conversations. But I deviate from how the authors describe them, particularly their causes and solutions.

different perspectives and ideas, as I describe in more detail in the chapter *Decision-Making and Negotiation*.[51]

Therefore, be accepting of the other person's perspective, even if you disagree. Don't assume that you are right, and resist the temptation to tell the other person that she or he is wrong. It's something you can train yourself to do. For example, I used to feel a strong urge to correct people when I first started to teach, and I consequently used to explain to the individuals why their thinking was flawed. But I've trained myself to be more accepting and to allow another person's perspective to exist without necessarily commenting on or correcting it. This makes the person feel heard, and it's often what's really needed to be able to move on.

Attachments

The longer we work on a product, the fonder we tend to become of it. The more we know, the more we usually view ourselves as experts and believe that we know best. As a consequence, we become attached to our views and ideas—we might even identify ourselves with them. For instance, when I was about to finish my book *Agile Product Management with Scrum*, the publisher suggested a final review of the draft manuscript. One of the people involved in this review was a well-known and valued colleague of mine. He went to great lengths to capture and share his comments, which I appreciated. But I found some of the comments so upsetting that I slept badly for a couple of nights.

What had happened? Writing a book—like any other new product development effort—requires a significant amount of time, energy, and dedication. It is therefore all too easy to become attached to what we believe the product should look like. I consequently took the feedback personally and saw it as a criticism of *myself* rather than of the book. Once I had calmed down, however, and I had overcome my resentment, I was able to discover helpful advice amongst the difficult

---

51   This is not to say that data are unhelpful. The opposite is true: Use data to make decisions, but be aware that it can be interpreted in different ways and that your interpretation is not necessarily the only valid one.

feedback, which helped me improve the book. Therefore, when you have a strong reaction to someone's opinion, use it as an opportunity for self-reflection: The cause for it is likely to be in yourself.

Desire to Win

Let me ask you a question: How do you usually get a pay raise and promotion? Most likely not for admitting that you were wrong and made an error. Many workplaces I have seen are competitive, and such an environment encourages competitive behaviour. This in turn fuels the desire to achieve and win, to be better than others and to outsmart them. If you are caught up in the desire to win, you are prone to suffer from confirmation bias—believing that you know best and that your ideas must be right. This can make it very hard to admit that another person's opinion is as valuable as yours and possibly even more helpful.

Problem-Solving Mode

Imagine that we are joining Kim, the person in charge of the product, in a product strategy workshop where the attendees—development team reps and key business stakeholders—discuss how to best evolve the product roadmap. Kim argues that retaining existing users is the right goal for the next quarter. But Bob, the sales rep, disagrees and pushes hard for addressing a new market segment. Faced with conflict, what should Kim do? A common solution would be to quantify the pros and cons of both options in order to find out which one is preferable and hence should be used. This seems the logical thing to do, right? But if Kim stood up, walked to the whiteboard, performed a cost-benefit analysis for both alternatives, and explained to Bob that her suggestion is factually better, then Bob would probably still find it difficult to agree with her. Why is that?

Our emotions play a major role in our lives and particularly in any conflict we experience. Disputes often evoke unpleasant feelings, such as irritation, frustration, anger, ill will, anxiousness, worries, and fear. You can think of conflict as an iceberg. What's visible are the verbalised thoughts, views, and opinions. Hidden underneath the surface are the emotions, together with the needs and interests of the individuals involved. Ignoring them makes it impossible to resolve conflict. Unfortunately, we can get so caught up in our thinking minds that we fail to pay attention to our feelings, which can cause us to act them out—for instance, by raising our voices and using harsh speech. How come? Acknowledging emotions is often seen as a sign of weakness and vulnerability, particularly in male-dominated work environments. What's more, we are taught how to think and reason from an early age. But we are not as much trained in recognising emotions and relating to them in a skilful, non-reactive way.

If, however, you don't attend to the emotions present when experiencing disagreement and instead jump into problem-solving mode, chances are that the other person will be held back by her or his feelings, resist your logic, and not be able to support your suggestions, even if they are objectively right: Treating disagreement as a purely intellectual issue does not do it justice. Instead, explicitly acknowledge the individual's feelings. In the example, Kim might say to Bob, "You seem very passionate about the idea of addressing a new segment. Can you please help me understand why that is?" This would make Bob feel understood and signal to him that Kim takes a real interest in what he has to say and why it is important to him.

Blame Game

When we experience conflict, we often focus on who is to blame, or who is at fault.[52] What's more, we routinely blame the other person for any difficult emotions we experience, like anger, worry, and fear. Let's say that Bob from the previous example is angry that his suggestion has not been taken up. He abruptly leaves the meeting and shouts

---

52   Avery (2016), Rosenberg (2015), Sofer (2018), and Stone, Patton, and Heen (2010) identify blame as a major barrier for overcoming conflict and growing as individuals and teams.

while storming out of the room, "Oh, you just do whatever you want with your product. You never take on other people's ideas anyway. I've really had enough!" Witnessing Bob's behaviour, Kim is likely to feel angry with him or worried about what else he might do, and she may well blame her anger or anxiety on Bob, thinking that it's his fault that she is feeling upset or worried.

But what did happen? Bob clearly behaved in an inappropriate way: He accused Kim of continued wrongdoing and shouted at her, thereby displaying signs of anger and aggression. But does this automatically mean that he intended to hurt Kim and wanted her to be miserable? It's more likely that Bob lost his temper and took his frustration out on Kim. But even if Bob intended to hurt Kim, blaming him and labelling him as a bad person would not be helpful. Instead, it would cause Kim to hold on to her anger. It might even lead her to retaliate and say something mean about Bob to the other workshop attendees, which she would later regret.

What's more, it is seldom one individual's fault. In this example, Kim's lack of empathy might have caused Bob to think that she doesn't value his opinion and care about him. Consequently, he might have felt hurt and rejected. This certainly does not justify Bob's behaviour. But it helps explain how the conflict developed, and it shows that both Bob and Kim contributed to it. Accepting responsibility and moving from a blame frame to a *contribution mindset*, thereby taking responsibility for their feelings and actions, will help the two individuals stop being caught up in a blame narrative, resolve the conflict, and repair the relationship (Stone, Patton, and Heen 2010, 79).

Artificial Harmony

Sometimes disputes aren't visible but are hidden underneath a blanket of artificial harmony. Let's revisit the preceding example and assume that Bob does not react as previously described. Instead of shouting at Kim and storming out of the meeting, he rolls his eyes, sighs, and says, "All right, then, it's your call, Kim." Relieved that the issue has been seemingly resolved, Kim continues to go through the agenda, while Bob remains silent for the remainder of the meeting. But has the disagreement really been cleared up? As long as Bob objects to Kim's approach, he won't be able to fully support it. Worse, he might hold a grudge against Kim, believing that she did not value his views and concerns. This would damage the relationship and make it hard to work together in the future. Sadly, I find it all too common that people opt for artificial harmony at work and habitually ignore or suppress conflicts instead of addressing them. Here are four reasons for this behaviour:

- *Fear of confrontation*: We are concerned that we will cause more harm by addressing the issue than letting it be, and we tell ourselves that if we don't deal with it, it will eventually go away or resolve itself (Sofer 2018, 65–66). Additionally, we may worry that resolving the conflict will make us vulnerable—we might not feel safe to admit that we made a mistake or have a weakness, or we might be uncomfortable talking about "fluffy stuff" like feelings and needs (Lencioni 2002, 63).
- *Wrong priorities*: We believe that addressing the conflict is not a high priority and that we should attend to other, more pressing matters. After all, there is so much *real* work that needs to be done, including reviewing the product roadmap and refining product backlog items. We really don't have the time to sort out all these pesky people issues.
- *Work culture*: Some organisations see conflict as a necessity for collaboration, innovation, and growth; others regard it as undesirable or even unacceptable. For example, when I was working at Intel, I felt that I could express my disagreement with senior stakeholders—challenging the status quo was an important part of the work culture at the company. But I have also worked with organisations that had strong hierarchies and an authoritarian leadership bias, where having meaningful disagreements and engaging in conflict was much more difficult and sometimes perceived as a sign of disrespect.
- *Lack of trust*: When people don't trust each other, they are not often able to address conflict but hide tensions and disagreements

(Lencioni 2002, 91–92). People consequently hold back their real opinions and honest concerns, are prone to make sarcastic comments, or complain about others behind their backs.

Unfortunately, ignoring conflict doesn't do us any favours. It results in mistrust, poor collaboration, low productivity, and lack of ownership—people who don't trust each other don't hold one another accountable for achieving shared goals (Lencioni 2002). What's more, we miss out on the creativity and innovation that constructive conflict can give birth to. As I explain in the chapter *Decision-Making and Negotiation*, encouraging divergent thinking and fostering diverse ideas is often a prerequisite for finding the right solution. Finally, think about the impact an unresolved conflict has on others. For instance, if the conflict between Kim and Bob is not properly addressed, then there is likely to be an awkward, unproductive atmosphere in the next meeting. The other participants may mince their words, and open, honest communication will be hard to achieve.

Resolve Conflict with Non-Violent Communication

Conflict can be a blessing or a curse depending on how we deal with it. If we learn to skilfully navigate it, disagreement will become a source of learning and creativity. *Non-violent communication* (NVC) is a simple yet effective framework developed by Marshall Rosenberg to resolve conflict. Its name indicates that our listening and speaking practices are particularly important when we experience conflict, and it suggests that true conflict resolution is only possible when we are willing to move beyond blame and ill will and have compassion for the other person and ourselves. It is therefore also called *compassionate communication*.[53]

---

53 Rosenberg (2015, Loc 354) uses the term *nonviolence* "to refer to our natural state of compassion when violence has subsided from the heart." Note that I discuss the importance of self-compassion in the chapter *Self-Leadership*.

Overview of the Framework

Non-violent communication consists of the following four components (see Rosenberg 2015, Loc 406, and Sofer 2018, 110):

Table 3: *The Four Components of Non-Violent Communication*

Component	You	The Other Person
Observations	What did you see and hear? Tell your story as objectively as you can, without judgement, blame, or criticism.	What is the other person's story? Attentively listen to the individual while refraining from evaluating and judging.
Feelings	How do you feel about it? Are you, for example, sad, hurt, irritated, angry, worried, or embarrassed?	What emotions is the other individual experiencing? How is she or he feeling?
Needs	Why do you feel the way you do? Which underlying needs are not being met? For instance, your need for respect, harmony, belonging, or safety.	Which unmet needs does the other person have?
Requests	What are the specific actions you would like to ask for in order to meet your needs and prevent the conflict from recurring?	What actions will help the other individual?

As table 3 shows, the NVC framework encourages us to establish a *dialogue* with the other person, share each other's perspectives, explore the feelings that are present, and connect them to underlying, unmet needs. This builds trust and understanding; it makes it possible to address the root cause of the conflict and to prevent it from erupting again.

Let's look at how the framework might be applied to the conflict between Bob and Kim, which I described earlier. After apologising for his behaviour, Bob starts the conversation:

Table 4: *A Sample Application of Non-Violent Communication*

Bob:	"This is how I experienced things: When you carried out a cost-benefit analysis in the meeting using data that seemed to favour your suggestion, I felt very angry."
Kim:	"I hear you, Bob. Now, when you shouted at me and said that I would never take on other people's ideas, I felt angry and embarrassed. But tell me, why did you get so upset and angry?"
Bob:	"I had the impression that you did not value my opinion, that you wanted to decide on your own how to evolve the product, particularly as I did not see you take on board any of my ideas in the previous roadmap workshop."
Kim:	"I see. I felt angry and embarrassed, and I want to be treated with respect. After all, I do want the product to be successful."
Bob:	"OK, I get it. How can we move on?"
Kim:	"I'd like to ask you to tell me in the future when you feel treated unfairly or ignored. I also want to ask you to treat me respectfully. Please continue to be honest and direct, but talk to me nicely. Is that OK?"
Bob:	"Yes, that's fair. In return, can you please be more inclusive, carefully consider what I have to say, and not quickly dismiss it?"
Kim:	"Yes, I'll make an effort to listen to you more carefully. I'll also clearly ask if anybody has any objections to product roadmap changes, and, if so, I'll take the time to address them."

Note that Rosenberg (2015) recommends using the following template when applying the framework:

Table 5: *Non-Violent Communication Template*

"*When I see / hear* [observation], *I feel* [emotion] *because I need / value* [need]. *Would you be willing to* [request]?"

In my mind, the specific choice of words is less important than the intention to understand the other person and amicably address the issue. To put it differently, if you diligently adhere to the template in table 5 but lack the right mindset, you are unlikely to successfully resolve the conflict.

Before You Start

Effectively addressing conflict is difficult when we are trapped in negative emotions and thoughts and when we hold a grudge against the other person, think of the individual as an opponent, or want to retaliate: Our state of mind influences how we perceive things and how we communicate. When you feel hurt or grumpy, for instance, your thoughts are likely to show negative discolouration, and you might interpret what others say as criticism rather than as their observation. For a constructive dialogue, it is therefore helpful to calm your mind, let go of adversarial thoughts and feelings, and be willing to forgive as well as to ask for forgiveness.

Let Go of Negative Emotions and Thoughts

While experiencing difficult emotions is normal in conflict, being caught up in them will make it hard to effectively apply the non-violent communication framework. I have found the following steps helpful to let go of difficult feelings like anger and ill will and to embrace a more open, warm-hearted attitude towards the other person:

1. *Look for positive qualities in the individual.* Think of something good the person has said or done and remind yourself of her or his positive qualities. This tends to soften any negative emotions and thoughts. It helps you to stop seeing the individual as an opponent or bad person, and it allows you to embrace a friendlier attitude towards the person. In the conflict between Bob and Kim, the latter might try to appreciate that Bob participated in the meeting and contributed to it, for example, or she might remember that Bob can be a friendly and caring colleague. Cultivating gratitude

will soften your attitude towards the individual and make you more accepting of her or his perspective and needs.[54]

2. *Stop reinforcing negative thoughts and emotions.* When you continue to have negative thoughts about the person, remind yourself that clinging on to them is not going to improve anything. Instead, it negatively affects your mental well-being: Projecting our anger and other unwholesome emotions on to another person is like throwing burning coal at someone. We may or may not hit the individual, but we will certainly hurt ourselves and burn our hand.[55] Even if anger, fear, or worries seem to have a tight grip on us, they will weaken and go away when we stop feeding them. Therefore, acknowledge them and let them be; try not to engage and identify with them.

3. *See things from the other person's perspective.* Ask yourself what might have caused the individual's behaviour. How did she or he experience the situation? What was it like for her or him? Disagreement and misunderstandings often arise because we are trapped in our view of the world, our experience based on our expectations. By reflecting on the other person's experience, we put our own version of reality into perspective and start to empathise with the individual.

Depending on how strong your emotions are, you may need some time to calm your mind, develop a less adversarial attitude, and be able to enter a meaningful dialogue with the individual. While you should not procrastinate in addressing the conflict—and possibly make the mistake of thinking that the issue will go away on its own—you also shouldn't put yourself under pressure to immediately resolve the conflict. Difficult emotions can take time to weaken and

---

54　Note that we can happily accept and disagree with what another person has said and done at the same time. Acceptance simply means recognising what is; it does not imply approval.

55　This quote is often attributed to the Buddha. But it may actually be from Buddhaghosa, as Bodhipaksa suggests. See fakebuddhaquotes.com/holding-on-to-anger-is-like-grasping-a-hot-coal-with-the-intent-of-harming-another-you-end-up-getting-burned.

disappear, and sometimes it is best to wait a day or two before trying to resolve the dispute.

Be Willing to Forgive and to Ask for Forgiveness

Conflict resolution is not about winning, retaliating, or putting the other person in her or his place. It's about developing a shared perspective on what happened, agreeing on the changes required, and re-establishing trust. This requires a willingness to forgive the other person and yourself (Amro 2018).

A technique that helps me practise forgiveness is to remind myself that whenever someone says or does something harmful, the individual cannot be truly happy. Instead, she or he must experience some form of distress. For example, I know from my own experience that when I use harsh or unkind speech, I am usually stressed, worn out, or in another unhappy state of mind. In other words, I act out my mental state, often without being fully aware of what's happening. Bringing to mind that the other person must be unhappy or distressed in some way helps me empathise with the individual and feel compassion for her or him. This allows me to be willing to forgive. If I find myself still clinging on to thinking that the person should pay for his or her behaviour, I tell myself that I am far from perfect and that I have acted in inappropriate ways and said unkind things. This weakens my righteous attitude, the idea that the other person must experience some suffering to make up for what she or he did. Additionally, I remind myself that I have made plenty of mistakes in my life, that I have said and done things I later regretted. This makes it easier for me to have empathy for the other person and be willing to forgive.

I use a similar approach to forgive myself, which is sometimes more difficult than forgiving someone else: We can be our hardest critics and full of self-judgement. But there is no point in beating ourselves up—just like there is no point in pretending that it's entirely the other person's fault. All we achieve is feeling more miserable. Acknowledge any wrongdoing, but do not allow it to define who you are. Have the courage to admit to it and apologise to the other person. Being able to admit a mistake is a sign of strength and maturity—not a weakness.

Share Observations

The first step to resolve conflict using non-violent communication is to clearly state what you saw happening and what you heard, as well as carefully listening to the other person's story.

While as product people we should be good at separating data from analysis, I often find it challenging to stick to my observations and not add any evaluations, judgements, or indirect criticism when sharing my story, particularly when I am still feeling angry or hurt. But as Sofer (2018, 75) rightly notes, "the less blame and criticism are in our words, the easier it will be for others to hear us." For example, if Bob said to Kim, "You are power-hungry and always ignore my suggestions," in the conversation in table 4, he would have labelled Kim as well as generalised and evaluated her behaviour rather than stating his observation. This would make it much harder for Kim to accept Bob's perspective. Fortunately, Bob stuck to the facts and said, "I did not see you take on board any of my ideas in the previous roadmap workshop." This message is free of any labelling, generalisation, and evaluation. It simply communicates Bob's observation. Therefore, be mindful of the words you choose, and stick to the facts.

But sharing your observation is only part of what needs to happen in the first step of resolving the conflict. The other, sometimes even more challenging aspect is to empathically listen while refraining from quickly judging, dismissing, and interpreting what you hear. As mentioned before, carefully listening to and accepting what the other person has to say does not mean that you agree with the individual or approve the message. Instead, it recognises that there is more than one perception of reality, more than one story, which is the prerequisite for empathising with and understanding the individual.

How we communicate is therefore particularly important when we are dealing with conflict.

The practices discussed in the chapter *Conversations* will help you express your story in a truthful way using kind words so that the other person can understand your perspective; they will also help you listen deeply and accept the individual's perspective.

Explore Feelings

Emotions play a key role in conflict: We can analyse the dispute and try to problem-solve as much as we want; as long as we are gripped by anger, fear, and other difficult emotions, we can't move on and make up with the other person. Nevertheless, we are not always good at paying attention to our feelings, particularly at work. We consequently ignore and suppress them, or, when it gets to be too much, we act them out. Bob, for example, may have bottled up his frustration with Kim's leadership style for a while until it finally erupted. If he had been more attentive to his inner life, he would have recognised the frustration building up and could have articulated his feelings in a constructive way at an earlier point in time—rather than flaring up at Kim.

Dealing with Difficult Emotions

When we experience difficult emotions, we are often tempted to blame them on the other person, as discussed before. But in order to resolve conflict, we must take responsibility for our feelings, thoughts, and actions. Bob, for example, may have triggered the feeling of anger and embarrassment in Kim. But these emotions belong to her, and she is responsible for skilfully dealing with them—understanding that they will weaken and eventually disappear if she recognises them and refrains from fuelling them by having unkind thoughts about Bob. Seeing what sets off our emotions and being attuned to our feelings allows us to avoid unhelpful, habitual reactions like Bob shouting at and accusing Kim—that is, showing the same reaction to the same triggers without being (fully) aware of what we are doing.[56]

While difficult emotions are unpleasant, they are part of our life. Everybody occasionally feels irritation, frustration, anger, worries, fears, and so on. Therefore, don't be self-judgemental, and don't beat yourself up for having negative feelings, but do relate to them in the right way. Don't hold on to or identify with them. Don't label yourself as an angry or anxious person, for example. Simply recognise instead that anger or fear is present—just like it is in millions of other people right now. Don't allow negative emotions to define you. By the same token, don't ignore and suppress them. Admit that you are, for instance, experiencing anger or anxiousness right now. Tell yourself that it's no problem as long as you don't reactively express your emotions or suppress them. Then take the next step and investigate what underlying cause the emotion is connected to.

Recognising Emotions

Even though noticing and accepting our emotions is important to resolve conflict, this is sometimes easier said than done: The ideas and beliefs we have about ourselves, who we want to be, and what we should or should not do can prevent us from recognising and accepting difficult emotions. For example, if Kim likes to think of herself as a kind and confident person, then it may be hard for her to accept that she feels anger and embarrassment. In other words, when the emotions present in us do not correspond to our self-view, we might subconsciously ignore and suppress them. Something similar can happen when we are stressed and tense: The tension we carry can cover our feelings and make it harder for us to notice them. If you find it difficult to recognise and accept your emotions, I recommend exploring the questions in table 6.

Make sure you don't rush through the questions in table 6. Take your time to answer them. Be aware that often several feelings are

---

56 Cultivating mindfulness as discussed in the chapter *Self-Leadership* will help you with this.

present that can be initially hard to discern. If that's the case for you, start with the most dominant one. Afterwards, look at the more subtle emotions. If you find, however, that you don't feel anything, then try to relax. You might be caught up in thoughts, or you might be numb from stress or tiredness. To get back in touch with your feelings, pay attention to your body: Look for areas where you feel discomfort or tightness—for example, in your face, belly, or chest—and try to soften them. This should help you unwind and become more aware of any emotions that are present. As the questions in table 6 indicate, feelings manifest themselves in the body.

Table 6: *Feeling Emotions, Taken from Sofer (2018, 145)*

Emotion	How do you feel?
Location	Where do you feel it?
Sensation	What does it feel like? Is there pressure, tightness, aching, heaviness? Warmth, openness, lightness, flowing?
Tonality	What's the overall flavour or tone of the emotion? Is it pleasant, neutral, or unpleasant?
Meaning	Are there any thoughts or stories connected with the emotion? If you had to describe it in one word, what would it be?
Needs	To which need is this emotion connected? What matters to you here?

Sharing Emotions

Once you are aware of your feelings, non-violent communication encourages you to share them. While this may require courage, it is necessary that you take this step: It helps the other person empathise with you and understand what impact her or his behaviour had on you—and vice versa. For example, Kim telling Bob that she felt angry and embarrassed in table 4 allowed Bob to see how his behaviour impacted Kim and hopefully learn from it. What's more, it helps Bob see Kim as a human being and allows him to gradually let go of his preconceived view of Kim as an arrogant, power-hungry product person. In other words, verbalising our feelings helps us move beyond labels and projections to see the humanity of the other person.

Uncover Needs

In non-violent communication, needs are considered to be at the root of our feelings; they are the real reason why we feel the way we do and why we want what we want (Rosenberg 2015; Sofer 2018). For instance, Bob might seek recognition, empathy, and possibly financial gain—he might want to maximise the chances of meeting his sales target and receiving a bonus. Kim might long for respect and trust. But she might also want to meet her personal objectives and receive a financial reward. As this example shows, it's not uncommon that our intentions are mixed and that different needs are at play.

The Role of Needs in Conflict

When there is conflict, we argue about seemingly opposing opinions, options, and ideas. At face value, these may simply be incompatible. For example, if there are no data available that clearly show whether user retention or acquisition is the right choice, Kim and Bob could argue forever without resolving the dispute and reaching agreement. In practice, they would probably compromise and, for instance, agree on a dual goal for the next quarter that combines both options. But as I discuss in the chapter *Decision-Making and Negotiation,* bargaining about positions is hardly ever the right thing to do: It usually results in a weak compromise that doesn't really benefit either party.

This is where needs come in: Needs like recognition, respect, trust, safety, and financial security are common to our human experience: We all have them to a certain degree, or at least we can relate to them. Understanding our mutual needs helps us discover that despite different opinions and views, difficult emotions, and possibly harsh words, the conflicted parties have a shared interest. This helps you to find a mutually agreeable solution, and it allows you to address the root cause of the conflict. This makes it less likely that the same issue will recur. What's more, by sharing needs, you cultivate empathy and build trust. These are the prerequisites for encouraging a behaviour change in the other person, as discussed in the chapter *Introduction*.

Learning and Growth

Uncovering your needs not only will help you resolve the conflict but also will allow you to learn something about yourself, including your deeply held values and beliefs. Kim might discover, for instance, that money is more important to her than she had previously thought, or she might find that connected to her legitimate need for respect is an insecurity about how she performs her role, which in turn is caused by the desire to succeed in her job. Similarly, hearing about the needs of the other person helps you better understand the individual and find out why the person reacted the way she or he did.

This enquiry necessitates, however, that we take full responsibility for our feelings and stop blaming others for our state of mind. It also requires the willingness to honestly reflect on your motives as well as taking a warm-hearted interest in the other person. You might find that your self-view can make it hard at times to see your needs, just like negative emotions will make it more difficult to be receptive to the needs of the other person. Kim, for instance, might initially struggle to admit to herself that achieving a personal financial gain is one of her goals, as she might like to think of herself as someone who is generous but not materialistic. Similarly, Bob will have a hard time appreciating Kim's need for respect if he still holds a grudge against her.

Make and Receive a Request

The final component of the non-violent communication framework is making a request and receiving what the other person is asking for. The conflict is considered resolved when both parties accept the other person's request, as Kim and Bob do in table 4.

Ask, Don't Demand

When you make a request, ensure that you ask and not demand. If Kim had said to Bob, for example, "Never shout at me or accuse me again," she would have demanded a behaviour change rather than asked for it. What's the big deal? First, as product people, we are usually not in a position to tell others what to do and to make demands. Second, if you try to make someone do what you want, you are not resolving the dispute—you are dictating a solution that the person may or may not agree with and that hence may create a winner and a loser. As much as you may want the other person to accept your request, be prepared that the individual will say no to it—just like you may decide to decline what the individual is asking for.

Make Your Request Clear, Specific, and Positive

Clearly say what you want, and ensure that your request is clear and specific. If the other person doesn't quite understand what you are asking for, then it will be hard for the individual to decide how to respond, and it will be difficult to effectively action it. For instance, if Bob had simply asked Kim to be more inclusive without qualifying what he means, Kim might have been unsure of what this entails. Consequently, she might have declined his request or not been able to action it as intended by Bob.

When formulating your request, use positive language and refrain from stating what you don't want (Rosenberg 2015, Loc 1499). For example, if Kim said to Bob, "Don't shout at me again," Bob might have interpreted the request as criticism, making it difficult for him to accept the message. The techniques discussed in the chapter *Conversations*, including *flipping* and *framing*, will help you articulate a positive request that the other person can receive.

Hearing and Saying No

After using the previously described components of non-violent communication framework, you will hopefully be able to accept each other's requests. But that's not always the case; sometimes the answer you hear is no. You might then feel disappointed, let down, or even angry. But don't give up yet. Continue the conversation by asking the individual to share her or his reasons for declining your requests. Ask what prevents the individual from saying yes and if the person has any other suggestions or ideas that would help address your needs (Sofer 2018, 203).

Alternatively, you might find that you have to decline what the other person is asking for—be it that it is incompatible with one of your needs or that you consider it inappropriate or wrong. Clearly explain why you cannot accept the request and offer to explore more options to find a solution that works for both of you (Sofer 2018, 204). With more time and enough goodwill, you will hopefully find a mutually agreeable solution that addresses the underlying needs of both parties and resolves the dispute.

When You Can't Resolve the Conflict

True conflict resolution is only possible if both parties are willing to co-operate—move beyond blame, take responsibility for their behaviour and feelings, and embrace a contribution mindset. Leading by example—empathetically listening to the other person, appreciating the individual's feelings, and taking a sincere interest in her or his needs—will hopefully help the individual open up and participate in the process. But there is no guarantee, of course, that she or he will follow your example and that the conflict will be successfully resolved. You can encourage change in another person, but you cannot *make* someone else change. Some people have simply acquired unhealthy habits that prevent them from constructively resolving conflict. Despite your best intentions, you may therefore not be able to settle the dispute. If that's the case, it's natural to feel emotions like disappointment and anger. But don't act them out, and don't threaten or try to coerce the other person. Instead, stop the process, talk to your line manager and HR, and consider involving a neutral and skilled mediator who can help resolve the conflict.

Helping Others Resolve Conflict

When you witness conflict between several stakeholders or a stakeholder and a dev team member and the individuals don't show any sign of successfully resolving the disagreement, don't ignore the situation.[57] A lingering conflict does not only affect the people involved but also impacts the rest of the group by reducing morale and productivity. Instead, try the following:

First, talk to the Scrum Master to share observations and to consult on how to best help the parties. The individual should be able to support you in addressing the issue; she or he might even be in a better position to help resolve the dispute.

Second, share your observations with the individuals involved in the conflict. Don't analyse or judge, don't assign fault or lay blame, and don't suggest a solution. State as objectively as possible what you have seen and heard. Explain what impact the conflict has on you and the rest of the group. Empathically listen to what the individuals have to say. You may want to do this by having a one-on-one conversation with each person or inviting the parties to a joint meeting, depending on what you believe will work best.

Third, consider offering to teach non-violent communication practices to the individuals so that they can resolve the conflict on their own. If this approach is unlikely to be successful, you might want to suggest mediation. The latter, however, requires that the people involved in the conflict are open to mediation and accept that a mediator will help them resolve the conflict and find a mutually agreeable solution. If you offer to mediate, make sure that you have sufficiently strong conflict resolution skills and that you are not biased towards one party or involved in the disagreement. Otherwise, the individuals won't regard you as neutral and impartial, and they won't trust you.

If people don't accept any help but are not able to skilfully settle the conflict on their own, consider escalating the issue and involving the line managers of the individuals and HR.

---

57 Note that it's the Scrum Master's responsibility to help resolve disagreements between development team members.

DECISION-MAKING AND NEGOTIATION

Determining who makes decisions in an organization is one of the best ways to understand who has the power—who is in control.
John A. Buck and Sharon Villines

As the person in charge of the product, you make a myriad of decisions—from shaping the product strategy to determining the product details. Some of these decisions can and should be taken by you, but others require the involvement of the development team and stakeholders to either decide together or, if that's not possible, to negotiate. This chapter shares the techniques to help you develop inclusive solutions and reach sustainable agreements.[58]

The Benefits of Collaborative Decision-Making

While you can usually make business-as-usual decisions on your own, complex and high-impact decisions are best made together with the development team and stakeholders: You typically require people's

---

58   This chapter builds on the work of Hartnett (2010) and Kaner et al. (2014).

expertise to help you tackle complex issues and make the right decisions, and you need strong support from the individuals for high-impact decisions, like extending your product's life cycle or retiring it early. Applied correctly, a collaborative decision-making approach offers the following benefits:

- *Better decisions*: Deciding together leverages the collective knowledge and creativity of the dev team and stakeholders. It helps you consider all viewpoints, thereby reducing the risk of wrong and biased decisions—for example, favouring options that confirm your own preconceived ideas and opinions (confirmation bias) or being focused on negative issues (negativity bias).[59] Collaborative decision-making does *not* mean, however, that everyone is super happy with every decision. Instead, it's about involving people, carefully listening to them, and understanding their perspectives and needs in order to make the right decision.

- *Stronger alignment*: A collaborative decision-making approach addresses the product leadership challenge of aligning people without having the power to tell them what to do. It allows individuals to contribute to decisions, and it ensures that they understand why the decisions were taken. Consequently, it creates stronger support and a heightened commitment to follow them through. What's more, including others in the decision-making process is a sign of healthy leadership; it prevents you from being perceived as a product dictator, an autocratic leader who wants to make all the decisions.

- *Increased motivation*: Involving the development team members and stakeholders in important decisions makes the individuals feel valued and respected. It empowers people and increases their

---

59 The correlation between diversity and effective decision-making has been well documented. Surowiecki (2004, 31), for example, writes, "If you can assemble a diverse group of people who possess varying degrees of knowledge and insight, you're better off entrusting it with major decisions rather than leaving them in the hands of one or two people."

motivation to work on the product—assuming that everyone had the opportunity to contribute and was listened to.

While deciding together can be challenging at times, consider the alternatives: You might make the decision on your own and then persuade people to agree with you, or you might broker a compromise between the various individuals by trying to address everyone's ideas and concerns. The first option is unlikely to result in committed, motivated individuals. Even if people follow through on the decision, they are unlikely to be committed and take ownership when issues occur. Instead, they may regard them as *your* problems and blame you. The second option carries the risk of trying to please everyone and agreeing on the smallest common denominator. But this is hardly a recipe for success.

Decide When to Decide

Effective decision-making means neither rushing nor procrastinating decisions. But that's sometimes easier said than done. Say some of your key performance indicators show a positive trend, but others are flat or declining. Consequently, you are unsure whether you should change the product strategy. What should you do? In a situation like this, it can be helpful to determine the *last responsible moment*. That's the point in time when the cost of delaying a decision outweighs the benefits of not making it.[60]

In this example, postponing a strategy change might give you more conclusive data, and you might know better which action to take. This makes not deciding right now appealing. But what about the drawbacks? If you waited another month, would you likely experience a market share loss or engagement decline? And how bad would this be? If the drawback of not taking the decision is greater than the benefit of keeping the options open and delaying it, then you should decide now. Otherwise, you should postpone the decision and wait for more data to be available. As this example shows, even if you cannot quantify the cost and benefits of delaying a decision, considering its impact is likely to help you decide when it's the right point in time to make the decision.

---

60 I explain in Pichler (2010) how the technique can be applied to making detailed product decisions.

Set Yourself Up for Success

Successful collaborative decision-making doesn't happen by chance. It requires the necessary preparation work and sufficient guidance during the decision-making process. This includes engaging the right people in the right way, bringing on board a facilitator, fostering a collaborative mindset, and establishing helpful ground rules.

Engage the Right People in the Right Way

To ensure that the right decision is made and that it receives the necessary support, carefully consider who should be involved in the decision-making process. If a decision has a big impact, then I recommend involving development team representatives, key stakeholders, and sponsors. Examples of big-impact decisions include creating or changing the product strategy, deciding to pivot or retire a product, and developing a new product roadmap or reworking an existing one, like replacing goals or changing important dates.[61]

Inviting representatives from the dev team allows you to leverage their knowledge and to take into account design and technology concerns. It also helps the individuals acquire the relevant knowledge and act as evangelists within the development team, thereby enabling the team to be more self-sufficient. The team reps may, for example, understand not only why it was decided to pivot but also what the new value proposition is or who the new users are.

Involving the key stakeholders—the players, as defined in the chapter *Interactions*—helps you understand their needs and take advantage of their expertise, for instance, their marketing and sales knowledge. At the same time, it ensures that the individuals understand the decision and secures their buy-in. Asking the management sponsor to attend takes the individual's perspective into account,

---

61   If you are unsure who the key stakeholders are, perform a stakeholder analysis—for instance, by using the power-interest grid introduced in the chapter *Interactions*.

makes it more likely to win the person's support for the decision, and enables the individual to explain it to her or his senior management colleagues.

If, however, the decision is tactical in nature and has a lower impact on the product and organisation, then involving the development team is usually enough. Examples include analysing user data; updating and prioritising the product backlog; removing, changing, or adding new items; creating new user stories or reworking existing ones; and selecting and agreeing on the sprint goal.

You might find that some people are hesitant to participate in the decision-making process. If that's the case, find out why that is and explain how contributing to the decision will help meet their needs and interests. Consider timeboxing the meeting, for example, to one hour, to make it easier for people to accept your invite. Schedule a follow-up meeting if you cannot make a joint decision within the allocated timebox. If the opposite is the case, and you find that you can hardly make a product decision without having to involve several people, then this can indicate an underlying issue. For example, I've seen companies in which product people had to ask senior managers to approve their product backlog prioritisation and businesses where a product person had to consult a subject-matter expert before being able to make a decision on a feature. In the first case, the individuals lacked the necessary empowerment. In the second case, the product people didn't have the knowledge required. If you find yourself in a similar situation, then identify and address the actual root cause rather than trying to optimise the decision-making process.

Finally, the more important a decision is, and the less people know and trust each other, the more beneficial it is to bring everyone together in the same room. This makes it easier to build trust, establish a shared understanding, and develop an inclusive solution. If that's not possible, hold the meeting via videoconference.

Employ a Dedicated Facilitator

Successfully deciding together can be challenging for groups, as you might have experienced, yourself. Some individuals might enjoy sharing their ideas so much that they won't stop talking, while others might be shy and reluctant to contribute, and senior members might expect that their suggestions are followed by everyone. It can therefore be beneficial to involve a dedicated, skilled facilitator who helps people embrace a collaborative mindset, encourages everyone to fully participate and prevents individuals from dominating, ensures that the group has chosen a clear decision rule, and guides everyone through the decision-making process.

A dedicated facilitator is particularly useful in the following two circumstances: First, the group is not familiar with collaborative decision-making; people might be used to the person in charge of the meeting or the most senior individual making the decision. Second, people don't trust each other, possibly because the individuals haven't worked together or the group hasn't gelled yet. Consequently, they may not feel safe to speak their minds or to disagree with other members, particularly senior ones.

I have found that it is not uncommon for the product person to act as the facilitator. This might be OK when you work with a cohesive group whose members know how to practise collaborative decision-making and who trust and respect each other. Otherwise, this setup is far from ideal: Effectively playing the facilitator role often requires the individual's full attention in order to keep the meeting on track and to ensure that everyone participates but that nobody dominates. That's difficult for you, as you also have to contribute to the decision, make suggestions, and raise concerns. Additionally, a facilitator has to be seen as neutral and fair—the person should not influence the decision. But as I just mentioned, you should participate in the decision-making process.

I therefore recommend separating the product and facilitator roles. To put it differently, *avoid facilitating as the person in charge of the product*. Instead, ask the Scrum Master to take on this role. If that's not possible, find another person with the necessary skills. This allows you to be a group member and to actively contribute to the decision without having to facilitate at the same time or, for example, encourage some people to contribute and ask others to be more receptive and less dominant.

Foster a Collaborative Mindset

As important as it is to involve the right people, deciding together becomes very difficult when the individuals don't embrace a collaborative mindset. If people act in selfish ways and want to maximise their personal gain, seek to dominate the discussion, or believe that they know best and their idea must win, it will be impossible to develop an inclusive solution and reach a sustainable agreement. To successfully decide together, the individuals will benefit from adopting a mindset that is based on the following three principles:[62]

1. *Full participation*: Everyone is willing to contribute, and everybody is heard. Nobody seeks to dominate or hijack the decision-making process. Everybody feels safe to speak her or his mind.
2. *Mutual respect and understanding*: People make an effort to attentively listen to each other and appreciate the other person's perspective, goals, and needs. The individuals intend to talk to one another kindly and to treat each other respectfully. See the chapter *Conversations* for more information.
3. *Open-mindedness*: The group members strive to keep an open mind, understanding that everybody holds a piece of the truth and that everyone's perspective matters. "Ideas should not be favoured based on who creates them," as Brown (2009, 73) puts it.

When people are generally used to teamwork, applying these principles should feel normal. But if the individuals struggle to be

---

62   The first two values are based on Kaner et al. (2014, 24).

team players, if they don't trust each other, or if they are stressed or under lots of pressure, then they may find it hard to embrace the right mindset. Consequently, people will benefit from encouragement and guidance. This includes having a facilitator present who skilfully reminds people of the right mindset and helps establish ground rules like the ones discussed in the next section.

Set Ground Rules

Ground rules are guidelines that help the participants treat each other respectfully; they ensure that everyone is heard and that nobody dominates. Setting ground rules is particularly helpful when you work with a new or changed group. Table 7 lists sample guidelines that you might want to use in your decision-making meetings. It can be helpful to copy them on a large piece of paper, put them up on the wall, and have them visible during the meeting so that you can easily refer to them. If you have a dedicated facilitator, the individual would usually suggest the rules and remind people to follow them when necessary.

Table 7: *Communication Guidelines for Collaborative Decision-Making*[63]

Always speak from a place of respect for others and assume good intentions on the part of the group members.
Respect differences of opinion and value the diversity of the group members.
Listen with an open mind; be receptive and refrain from making premature judgements.
Speak honestly and openly. Always stick to observable facts.
Refrain from judging and labelling people; separate individual and opinion.
Ask questions when you sense misunderstanding or disagreement.
Speak up if you have not been participating.
Make room for others if you have spoken often.
Do not interrupt others, but allow a brief moment of silence to let the previous speaker's words sink in before the next person speaks.
Stay present; do not engage in side conversations or answer messages on your electronic devices.

---

63   The guidelines are based on Hartnett (2010, Loc 1297).

Note that introducing the best ground rules is of little benefit if you don't show a collaborative mindset and if you don't follow the rules. Therefore, be a role model and exhibit the behaviour you want to see in others. Listen empathically, speak truthfully and kindly, and make an effort to be open-minded. I once worked with a product person who was very knowledgeable and had great arguments for the decisions he made. Despite his expertise, people didn't support his decisions. How come? While he paid lip service to teamwork and collaborative decision-making, he didn't walk his talk. Instead, he came across as arrogant and close-minded.

Choose a Decision Rule

Imagine that you ask the development team and stakeholders at the end of a product strategy workshop, "Is everyone OK with changing the release goal for Q3?" Because nobody says anything, you assume that everyone agrees with your suggestion. You thank people for attending and close the meeting. But in reality, most individuals are still thinking about the change proposed. To make things worse, it's not clear who has the final say on product roadmap changes. Is it you, the people present, or the management sponsor?

Choosing a decision rule avoids these issues. Such a rule clearly states who decides and how you can tell that the decision has been made. For example, if you choose to decide by majority, then the entire group votes on the proposal. If more than half of the votes are in favour of it, the proposal is accepted, and a decision has been made. It is therefore important that you select the right decision rule and that everybody involved in the decision-making process understands it.

There are four common decision rules that facilitate group decisions: *unanimity*, *consent*, *majority*, and *product person decides after discussion*. Note that each rule has its strengths and weaknesses; none is always appropriate, as I explain next. In addition to these four participatory rules, I also discuss the following two additional decision rules: *product person decides without discussion* and *delegation.*

Unanimity

Deciding by unanimity means that everyone required to make the decisions agrees with the proposed solution and is happy to support it. This creates strong buy-in and shared ownership, and it leverages the collective creativity and knowledge of the people present—everybody involved contributes to the decision. Please note that *unanimity* and *consensus* are not synonyms. The former means that everyone agrees; the latter refers to reaching some form of agreement.[64]

Applying this decision rule is particularly helpful when the stakes are high and you make a strategic product decision that requires the support of the development team and stakeholders—for example, deciding to pivot or kill a young but unsuccessful product. On the downside, it can take a comparatively long time to reach unanimity, as it requires developing a mutual understanding and finding a proposal everyone involved in the decision-making process is happy with. What's more, unanimity is the decision rule that requires the highest level of engagement and collaboration. It can hence be the most difficult one to apply when people find it hard to be team players or don't trust each other.

A common challenge when deciding by unanimity is to understand whether there is enough support for a proposal and the group is ready to make a decision. A great technique to uncover the level of people's support is using an agreement scale like the one in table 8.

Table 8: *Sample Agreement Scale*

5	4	3	2	1
I wholeheartedly endorse the proposal.	I endorse it with minor reservations.	It's not great, but I support it.	I don't support it.	I have serious disagreements.

---

64 I follow Hartnett (2010) and Kaner et al. (2014), who define *consensus* as the process that helps people reach agreement.

The scale in table 8 shows five gradients of agreement, ranging from wholehearted endorsement to serious disagreement. You can, of course, use more gradients if you wish to, but I find that in practice, the five options in table 8 are usually enough.

With your scale in place, ask everyone how much they agree. A technique commonly used on agile teams is called *the fist of five*. Individuals express their agreement by showing the appropriate number of fingers—for example, five fingers for wholehearted endorsement and one finger for serious disagreements. Alternatively, you can use dot-voting. Ask people to draw a dot underneath the appropriate number. The resulting picture nicely visualises the group's level of agreement. Note that when using unanimity, people must explicitly express their support for the proposal. It would be a mistake to assume that silence signals agreement. Instead, see it as a sign that the group members need more time to think or don't feel comfortable to speak up. If nobody is in the one to two range and most people are in the four to five range using the scale in table 8, then you have a proposal that the group sufficiently supports, and a unanimous decision has been reached.

When using unanimity, allow for enough time to find an agreeable solution. Be patient and don't pressure people to agree. If, however, you are out of time and a decision must be made, you can consider changing the decision rule to *product person decides after discussion*, for example. Do make sure, though, that everybody understands why the change occurs. Do not use it to avoid difficult discussions or to force your will on to the group.

Additionally, don't allow unanimity to degenerate into *design by committee*, where people agree on the smallest common denominator and broker a weak compromise in order to shortcut the decision-making process or maximise their own gain. This is unlikely to result in a sustainable agreement and translate into a successful product. As the saying goes, "A camel is a horse designed by a committee."

Consent

Consent is the absence of objections: A decision is made when nobody disapproves.[65] Deciding by consent requires that a proposal has been created—either as part of the decision-making process or by delegating the task to a group of people. To use this decision rule, discuss the proposal and establish a shared understanding so that everybody is clear on its benefits and drawbacks. Then ask the participants to clearly state if they object or consent to the proposal. If there are objections, ask people to explain why they disagree. Then amend the proposal or ask a group of people to rework it. Iterate these steps until everyone involved in the decision-making process can live with the proposal and no longer has any meaningful objections.

Applying this decision rule is beneficial when you don't have the time to decide by unanimity or a good enough solution is sufficient. Remember the product roadmap story I mentioned earlier? Using consent would have been a great way to understand if the development team and stakeholders agree with the proposed roadmap change. Notice, however, that not objecting to a proposal does not necessarily imply that people are happy to support it. Consent therefore requires not giving you the same level of support as *unanimous agreement* does.

When deciding by consent, be careful not to shortcut the decision-making process by subtly pressuring people to agree or by not considering all meaningful objections. For consent to work, everyone involved in the decision-making process must be happy to speak up and to voice concerns or disagreement—no matter which role the person plays or how junior the individual might be.

Majority and Supermajority

As its name suggests, majority vote means that more than half of the people are required to agree with a proposed solution. Supermajority

---

65   This section is based on Buck and Villines (2017).

requires a greater agreement and more support than majority—for example, two-thirds or 75 per cent.

Applying the two rules is simple and fast. Unfortunately, it creates a win-lose situation that can leave the minority frustrated and unwilling to support the decision. To make things worse, using this decision rule can lead to people forming factions and fighting against each other in order to win, which is the opposite of what you would like to achieve in a collaborative decision-making process. I therefore recommend that you use majority and supermajority when the stakes are not high and when the proposal and its impact are clearly understood. Asking people to vote on a major strategy change would not be desirable in my mind; using unanimity or consent would be more helpful.

If, however, you cannot agree on a lower-impact issue—for instance, if a technical or user-related risk should be addressed in the next sprint—then you may want the Scrum team members to cast their votes. This speeds up the decision-making process and gets sprint planning done within its allocated timebox, and it's acceptable because the decision's impact is likely to be limited. You'll discover at the end of the next sprint if you've addressed the wrong risk, and in the worst case, you will have lost a sprint.

Product Person Decides after Discussion

This decision rule requires you to have an open discussion with the development team and stakeholders, where the participants share their perspectives. Once everybody has been heard and a shared understanding of the different ideas and concerns has been established, you make the decision as the person in charge of the product. This approach offers two main benefits: First, you retain control over the decision despite involving others in it. Second, it speeds up the decision-making process: *Person decides after discussion* tends to be quicker than unanimity and consent, as you don't have to find an inclusive solution or resolve all objections.[66]

The decision rule's drawback is that people may not support your decision—or worse, they might be frustrated and oppose it if they don't feel understood or if their suggestions were not taken on board. And if the decision turns out to be wrong, people may regard it as your mistake and blame you. What's more, the rule requires you to have the authority to make the decision, which might not be the case, particularly for high-impact decisions that affect revenue and other business goals.

Apply this rule when you need to involve the development team and stakeholders to benefit from their knowledge or to make them feel valued but you must make the decision rather than allowing the group to reach agreement. This can be necessary for three reasons: First, the individuals don't have enough product and market knowledge to be equal decision-making partners. This is often the case when you work with a new development team. Second, speed is more important than reaching a sustainable agreement and generating buy-in—for instance, in a crisis. Third, people are not showing a collaborative mindset and don't engage in a constructive way. Say you are coming to the end of the sprint review meeting and people are still arguing over the changes they would like to see without being able to reach agreement. Then you should stop the decision-making process and make a decision. This allows the meeting to reach closure and the development team to continue working.

When using the decision rule, apply the following three recommendations: First, make sure that you apply the listening techniques discussed in the chapter *Conversations*. Give each participant your full attention, listen for people's underlying needs and interests, and keep an open mind—no matter if you agree with the suggestions or

---

66 But this does not imply that you should not try to remove objections or find an inclusive solution. Carefully listening to the people present and building a shared understanding of their needs will allow you to recognize if that's possible or not, and it will show the group members that you value their perspectives and care for their needs.

not. If people don't feel understood, it will be hard for them to support your decision without feeling resentment or irritation, especially if they disagree. Second, make an effort not to favour anybody's ideas. Clearly explain the reasoning behind your final decision and base it on observable facts. Otherwise, people may not feel valued. Instead, they might feel resentment towards you and oppose the decision. Third, be careful not to overuse the decision rule. If you find that the development team and stakeholders always end up arguing or that the team members' product and market knowledge continue to be poor, then investigate and address the root causes. Maybe you need to involve a skilled facilitator or revisit the ground rules, and maybe you should help the dev team acquire the relevant knowledge—for example, by inviting its members to observe and interview users or to work on the product backlog with you.

Disagree and Commit

When I was working at Intel in the late 1990s, a common way to decide was to ask people to *disagree and commit*. This meant that after a discussion had taken place and individuals had had the opportunity to make suggestions and express concerns, the person in charge would make the decision. Everyone, even people who opposed it, would be asked to commit to it—that is, accept it and follow it through. When you apply the decision rule *product person decides after discussion*, you essentially ask the attendees to disagree and commit. But as I pointed out earlier, people are unlikely to support your decision if they don't feel heard and understood. I'd like to therefore stress again how crucial it is that you take a genuine interest in the individuals and empathically listen to them. If people don't feel understood and appreciated, they are unlikely to buy into your decision. Instead, they might follow it out of obligation, or they might ignore or even oppose it. But none of those actions makes it likely that the desired outcome will be achieved.

Product Person Decides without Discussion

As the person in charge of the product, you don't have to involve others in all your decisions, of course: There are lots of low-impact decisions you can and should make on your own. For example, should you invite the sales rep to the next sprint review meeting? Should you now start breaking down some of the larger epics in the product backlog or wait for another sprint? Should you move from monthly strategy and roadmap reviews to quarterly ones (or vice versa)?

Be aware, though, that this decision rule will only be helpful when you have the necessary expertise to make the decision and you don't need input from the development team or stakeholders. Take the example of changing the frequency of the product strategy reviews. If you are confident that you can make the right decision on your own and that the stakeholders will agree with you, then just decide. Otherwise, choose a participatory rule like consent. Avoid applying the rule for important decisions. Otherwise, people may regard you as a product dictator and oppose your decisions.

Delegation

Delegate a decision if others are better qualified to decide or if your input is not needed. As the person in charge of the product, you typically expect the development team to take care of all technical decisions. But you might also delegate decisions related to writing and refining user stories to the team, assuming that the team members have enough knowledge about the users and product and that the individuals are happy to take on the task.

Delegation ensures that the best-qualified people decide, and it frees up your time: You don't spend more time making decisions than necessary. When applied correctly, it also sends a positive signal to the appointed decision makers: It shows that you trust them and value their expertise.

But be careful not to use the rule to avoid difficult decisions. It can be all too easy to delegate a decision that you don't want to make. Additionally, do not try to influence the group tasked with making the decision. For example, it would not be appropriate to say, "You decide what the right software architecture is, of course. But I think we should use a service-oriented architecture." People are likely to interpret this message as a sign of mistrust or an attempt to influence their decision. If you need to be involved in the decision, then do not delegate it to others, but participate in the decision-making process.

Take the Right Decision-Making Steps

If you are like me, you'll want decisions to be made quickly: Get together, discuss the issue, brainstorm solutions, choose one, and move on. While there is nothing wrong with being decisive and wanting to progress things, the approach stated only works for business-as-usual decisions where agreement can be quickly reached. But if you want to leverage the collective wisdom of a group to decide on a complex or high-impact issue, you need to give people more time. The group members first have to share their perspectives and understand each other's ideas, concerns, and needs before a decision can be made, as figure 4 shows.

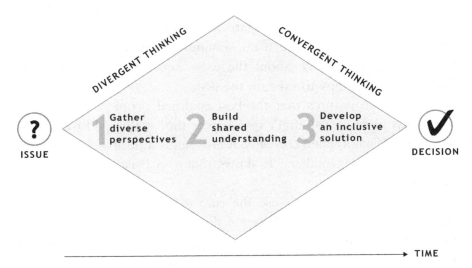

Figure 4: *A Collaborative Decision-Making Process Based on Kaner et al. (2014)*

The extent to which you execute the last step in figure 4 will depend on the decision rule you use. For example, when you apply *product person decides after discussion*, you are likely to spend less time and effort trying to come up with an inclusive solution compared to using *unanimity* as the decision rule. Independent of the decision rule applied, always collect different perspectives and create a shared understanding of people's needs and interests before you critique and discard ideas. Otherwise, you may end up with a suboptimal or wrong decision and not enough support from the dev team and stakeholders. In other words, clearly separate divergent thinking and generating ideas from convergent thinking, which involves evaluating, discarding, and combining ideas.

Step 1: Gather Diverse Perspectives

Start the process by making sure that everybody clearly understands the issue to be addressed. Then invite people to share their perspectives, come up with ideas, and voice any concerns they might have. It is essential that everyone has the opportunity to contribute and is listened to. This makes people feel valued and involved, and it allows you to collect different ideas and perspectives. A great technique to achieve this is structured brainstorming: Ask people to write their ideas on adhesive notes, briefly explain them, and then put them on the wall. Request that people refrain from analysing, judging, and criticising, and allow only clarification questions at this stage. Ideally, people feed off each other's ideas—one suggestion sparks another one.

Resist the temptation to shortcut the process and to prematurely reach agreement at this step. Otherwise you may end up with a mediocre solution based on familiar options. In the worst case, you experience *design by committee,* where people broker a weak compromise—which is the opposite of what a collaborative decision-making process should achieve.

Groupthink: Dealing with a Lack of Divergent Perspectives

Groupthink happens when the need for harmony or conformity prevents a group of people from making effective decisions. The members shy away from disagreement and conflict, avoid expressing disagreeing views, and consequently make suboptimal or wrong decisions.

One of the reasons of groupthink is a lack of trust amongst the group members. People who don't trust each other often create artificial harmony, where nobody speaks their minds and expresses disagreement. Instead, the members pretend to agree and share their disagreement behind each other's backs. If that's the case, consider how you can build trust and increase psychological safety. For example, you may want to voice disagreement while at the same time showing a sincere interest in the perspectives and needs of the other individuals. You might also find that making a confidentiality agreement, such as, "What is said in the room stays in the room," helps people open up and say what they really think.[67]

Another groupthink reason is the opposite of what I just described: The longer and better people work together, the fewer diverging perspectives you might hear; the group members develop shared ideas and make common assumptions. In this case, you might want to encourage creative and critical thinking, for example, by using de Bono's *six thinking hats* (de Bono 2016) or playing devil's advocate and intentionally arguing against a position in order to help determine its validity and foster debate. You might also find that following Steve Blank's advice to "get out of the building" and visiting users and customers helps the group question their assumptions and develop new ideas (Blank 2009). If this doesn't work, consider carefully adapting the group composition, for instance, by adding new members and increasing the diversity within the group.

Step 2: Build Shared Understanding

Once everybody has contributed and been listened to, take the next step and create a shared understanding. Often people assume that one idea or perspective must be right and should therefore be selected. This can lead to conflict and arguments, premature selection of a suggestion, and alienation of those who oppose the idea. To avoid this danger, help people understand where they are coming from and encourage them to explore the needs and interests behind people's

---

67 I discuss trust building in the chapter *Interactions* and avoiding artificial harmony in the chapter *Conflict*.

perspectives. For example, ask the individual to explain why an idea is important to them or why they feel strongly about a suggestion. What are the underlying motives or concerns?

Say you launched a new product four months ago. Unfortunately, the uptake is not great; the product is underperforming. You are now in a product strategy workshop discussing different ideas to move the product forward. One of them is to pivot by unbundling a major feature; the other one is to change the marketing strategy and increase the marketing effort. To help the group develop a shared understanding, you should not only discuss the benefits and drawbacks of the individual ideas, including any data or observable facts that support them, but also explore what motivated the individuals to come up with the two suggestions. What's in it for them? Why are the suggestions important for them personally? It might turn out that the individual who suggested the pivot never fully agreed with the original product strategy or that this would allow the person to contribute more and feel needed and useful.

Caring for people's needs not only builds shared understanding but also makes them feel valued and understood, even if their ideas turn out to be unhelpful, and it strengthens the connections amongst the group members. But it requires that the individuals keep an open mind, attentively listen to each other, and respect one another's ideas, needs, and concerns. Give the group the time needed to develop the shared understanding, and don't rush this step. If people don't understand each other sufficiently, then it will be very difficult, if not impossible, to come up with a solution that everybody can accept or at least understand.

Step 3: Develop an Inclusive Solution

Once the group has established a shared understanding and people know the reasoning and motivation behind the different suggestions, you are ready to develop an inclusive solution. But this does not mean that you should try to please everyone by cobbling together different ideas, nor does it entail brokering a compromise or agreeing on the smallest common denominator. A truly inclusive solution addresses the needs of everyone present and results in a sustainable agreement—a decision that people will follow through on. As mentioned before, the decision rule used will determine how inclusive the solution is: *Unanimous agreement* requires you to find a proposal everyone is happy with, *consent* means developing a decision nobody objects to, and *product person decides after discussion* may mean that you don't opt for an inclusive solution but instead ask people to follow your decision.

Don't Wait for the Perfect Solution

The desire to make only correct decisions can make you hesitant and cause you to unnecessarily prolong the decision-making process. While it's great to care about the decisions you make, don't search for the perfect decision. Instead, choose a good enough decision that allows you to move on. Then reflect on the outcome and revise the decision, if necessary. Innovation is not possible without taking risks and experiencing failure. Therefore, dare to fail. Be open to the possibility that despite your best intentions, you might make the wrong product decision. As Thomas Edison, the creator of the first commercially successful electric light bulb, famously said, "If I find 10,000 ways something won't work, I haven't failed. I am not discouraged, because every wrong attempt discarded is another step forward."

To develop an inclusive solution, start by considering how you can address people's needs, interest, and concerns while at the same time moving the product in the right direction. Would it be helpful to combine different proposals? Could you unbundle a feature and increase the marketing effort for the newly created product, to continue the earlier example? The best solutions often emerge when elements of different ideas are merged. If an integration is not possible or desirable, evaluate the different suggestions. Explore, for example, if there are any data that allow you to infer that pivoting or unbundling would be preferable. If that's not the case, consider stopping the discussion and carrying out experiments that test the two options following the motto *stop arguing, start experimenting*. For instance, you might want to carry out user interviews or develop throwaway prototypes to test the options and validate your assumptions. Then reconvene and continue the discussion until you have a proposal that people agree on and a decision can be made.[68]

Tips for Negotiating Successfully

"Listen, I really need you to add this feature to the release, and I am not going to take no for an answer," says Sophie, the head of sales, as she stands in front of your desk. You can feel your shoulders tensing and your stomach tightening. There is no way that you can add more work to the development effort—the dev team is already struggling with the current workload. But Sophie is a powerful senior manager who will not be afraid to escalate the issue. What should you do?

Despite your best efforts to involve people in the decision-making process, some individuals may not embrace a collaborative mindset but approach you with specific requests or demands. Consequently, you might find yourself negotiating—trying to resolve points of difference and aiming to reach agreement. The practices discussed in this section will help you with this. They are based on two well-known negotiation frameworks, the *principled negotiation method* and the *behavioural change stairway model.*[69]

A Brief Overview of the Principled Negotiation Method and the Behavioural Change Stairway Model

The *principled negotiation method* was created by William Ury and Roger Fisher as part of the Harvard Negotiation Project at Harvard University. First published in 1981 and refined in subsequent publications, the method recognises four aspects for successful negotiation (Fisher and William 2012):

---

68 For more information on research and validation, see Pichler (2016, *Strategize*).
69 If you haven't done so, then I recommend reading the chapters *Conversations* and *Conflict*, as they will provide you with the foundations to successfully negotiate. Negotiation essentially is a difficult conversation where conflict is present.

1. *People*: Separate the people from the problem.

2. *Interests*: Instead of arguing over positions, look for shared interests and needs.

3. *Options*: Invent multiple options, looking for mutual gains, before deciding what to do. Avoid the mistake of prematurely excluding options and opting for one solution.

4. *Criteria*: Use objective criteria or a fair standard to determine the outcome.

The *behavioural change stairway model*, first discussed in the chapter *Introduction*, proposes the following five stages that intend to take the negotiator from listening to influencing the behaviour of the other person (Voss 2016):

1. *Active listening*: Make an effort to empathically listen to the other person while suspending judgement.

2. *Empathy*: Understand the individual's perspective, needs, and interest, thereby accepting that emotions play a major role in how we behave as human beings.

3. *Rapport*: Build rapport and establish trust.

4. *Influence*: Help the other person let go of her or his position, understand your needs, and look for a solution that addresses the individual's needs at least partially.

5. *Behavioural change*: Agree on an acceptable solution that can be implemented (if possible).

Both frameworks capture the insight that negotiation is not about getting the better of the other person, nor is it about being confrontational or aggressive. Instead, it requires the willingness to attentively listen to the other party, understand her or his perspectives and needs, and build trust.

Cultivate a Friendly Attitude

When you find yourself in a situation as in the previous example, it's normal to experience negative emotions and to feel confused, worried, or angry, for instance. Consequently, you might feel the urge to fight back, tell Sophie what you think of her behaviour, and show a confrontational attitude. But negotiation is not about putting the other person in her or his place; it's not about getting the better of the other party, and it's not about winning and getting your way. Instead, it is about jointly solving a problem, no matter whether you like and agree with the other person. A confrontational approach never achieves a positive, mutually agreeable, and sustainable outcome. Instead, it results in bruised feelings and resentment. But you should therefore try to develop a friendly, warm-hearted attitude towards the other person along the lines described in the chapter *Conflict*. Otherwise it will be impossible to understand the individual, build rapport, and develop a mutually agreeable solution.

Fortunately, you don't have to agree with or like the other person to feel empathy, accept the position, and understand the individual's needs. Acknowledge any negative feelings and thoughts that you might have, but don't hold on to them. To overcome them, bring to mind the individual's positive qualities and the good things the person has said and done. For example, Sophie may be pushy at times, but she does care for her staff. Additionally, remind yourself that aversion, ill will, and anger reduce your mental well-being, distort your perception of reality, and make it hard to connect with others and build rapport. You can take this a step further by appreciating the person's effort to share the request with you and then wholeheartedly thanking the person, even if you disagree with the request. Cultivating gratitude will automatically soften your attitude towards the individual and make you more appreciative of her or his needs.

Overcoming negative emotions and thoughts and developing a friendly, warm-hearted attitude is key to building *trust*, and the degree to which the negotiating parties trust each other is a major factor in determining whether a negotiation is successful or not.

Listen Deeply

It's all too easy to be wrapped up in your own position and to come up with arguments to support it. For instance, you might think of how to convince Sophie that her request is unrealistic and not appropriate and determine a strategy to convince or even persuade Sophie. While this reaction is understandable, it is not helpful: It reaffirms your own beliefs and reduces your ability to be receptive and to understand Sophie's perspective. Instead of defending your position and trying to convince Sophie that you are right, first carefully listen to what she has to say.

Let go of your own position and arguments for now and give your full attention to the individual. Embrace a mindset of discovery and try to suspend judgement. Treat the other person with respect. Take an interest in what she or he has to say and what the underlying motives are. Be patient and don't interrupt the individual, disagree with her or him, or make your request while she or he is talking, as discussed in the chapter *Conversations*. Try to have a face-to-face conversation whenever you negotiate. If that's not possible, have a video call. This allows you to perceive important nonverbal cues. For example, Sophie might be red-faced while talking to you or raise her voice, which are likely to indicate that she is upset or angry.

Making an effort to empathically listen shows Sophie that you care about what she has to say. It allows you to empathise with her and to find out why adding the feature is important to her, and it builds trust, which you will need as much of as possible to negotiate successfully.

Don't Bargain over Positions

Faced with Sophie's request, it may be tempting to split the difference and offer a partial implementation of the feature to Sophie. But would this really be beneficial and lead to a lasting agreement? Or would it be a bad deal that doesn't address Sophie's real needs while making it more unlikely to complete the software on time and on budget?

In any difficult conversation, there is more than what is being said. While Sophie's request is important, understanding *why* she wants to add the feature is even more significant. Therefore, make an effort to understand the other person's underlying needs and interests and do not bargain over positions. For example, you might want to say to Sophie, "Thank you for telling me about the feature. Adding the feature now seems to be very important to you. Can you please help me understand why that is?" This helps you not only understand Sophie better but also enables you to come up with alternative solutions that address her needs as well as your own. There are four conversation techniques that are particularly helpful when negotiating (Voss 2016):[70]

- *Mirroring* and *positive reinforcement*: Repeat the exact same words in a warm and accepting voice, no matter if you agree with what was said or not. This provides you with three benefits: First, it ensures that you heard correctly what Sophie said. Second, it plays the message back to the sender and allows her to reflect on it. Third, it shows that you take an interest in what Sophie has to say and builds rapport.
- *Labelling*: Listen for the other person's emotions and call them out. You might say, for example, "You sound concerned. Is that right?" or "I sense that you are upset." You thereby acknowledge the individual's emotions and show that you understand and take an interest in how she or he feels. This builds trust and encourages the other person to reflect on how she or he is feeling.
- *Open-ended questions*: Ask open-ended questions to uncover the other person's needs, as suggested before. Say, for example, "Please help me understand how this would be beneficial." Similar to labelling, this shows that you are interested in understanding Sophie, and it builds rapport.
- *Patience*: Be patient and take the time to attentively listen to the individual. Don't interrupt the other person and don't try to rush the conversation. Otherwise, it will be hard to understand Sophie's underlying needs and motives. If you don't have time to listen to her, then thank her for raising the request and ask Sophie to schedule a follow-up meeting to properly discuss the matter.

Additionally, don't forget to reflect on your own needs and interests. You might find that there are several needs present: For instance, the need to be treated with respect; the need to honour a product

---

70   For more listening and speaking techniques, see the chapter *Conversations*.

roadmap, which was agreed by the stakeholders, development team, and yourself; and possibly the need to claim a bonus by meeting the agreed release goal on time and on budget. Using intentional silence can buy you the time required to determine your needs. Ask Sophie, for example, to give you a minute to think about what you have heard. A great guide to your needs is your emotions: Becoming aware of them and asking yourself why they are present will usually lead you to your needs.

Develop Options Together

Once you understand the *why*, you can explore alternatives to the initial positions and possibly even find a better solution. Let's say you've discovered that Sophie has requested the feature to win a new customer contract, which would allow her group to meet their ambitious overall sales targets. Equipped with this knowledge, you can start to explore alternative solutions that address Sophie's needs without impacting the current release. For example, you might suggest delaying the feature to the subsequent version but putting it on the product roadmap, you might explore changing a feature of the release to make the product version more attractive for the prospective customer, or you might investigate if and how you can maximise the sales from the product version without having to win the contract.

But don't think of this step as finally getting your way. Your job is to help Sophie let go of her fixed position and to become more open-minded and appreciative of your needs while helping her achieve or at least move forward towards her objective. Asking focused, *open-ended questions* will help you with this. For example, you might say, "How can I help you meet the sales targets without negatively impacting the release?" "What else could help you meet the sales targets?" or "How can we solve this problem together?"

Additionally, make sure that the solution you develop is fair—that it honours Sophie's and your needs. Agree with Sophie on a set of impartial criteria, such as impact on sales, delivering the release goal, and adhering to the budget and time constraints, and use the criteria to determine if a solution fair or not.

Reach Closure

Once you've selected a solution, check that Sophie is indeed satisfied with it. Explicitly ask her if she agrees, and don't ignore any hesitation in her voice or other nonverbal cues that indicate that she may not be happy. Instead, address them by saying, for example, "It seems you're hesitant. Please tell me what you are uncomfortable with. I want to make sure that we get this right." Additionally, consider if you need others to agree to the proposed solution. If, for example, product roadmap changes are collaboratively decided, then you should discuss the solution with the stakeholders and dev team members before you commit to it. Otherwise, Sophie might be happy with the solution, but the stakeholders and dev team might oppose it.

Ideally, you will have found a solution that addresses Sophie's needs and your own—a *win-win* solution. As you have developed a mutual understanding of your needs and created a solution together, you have not only solved the problem but also established trust and strengthened the relationship. How cool is that? Unfortunately, negotiations don't always end up with a mutually agreeable solution. There is no guarantee that you will be able to influence the individual and instigate a change in her or his behaviour. We can only encourage change in other people. But we can't *make* them change. For example, Sophie might not be willing to let go of her position; she might be confrontational and play a power game despite your best effort to empathise with her.

While it is important that you approach any negotiation with a friendly and positive mindset, you should not be desperate to strike a deal. Don't allow the other person to put you under pressure or threaten you, for example, by imposing a deadline and running down the clock. What's more, don't agree to a bad deal. No deal is often better than a bad one. Instead, you might opt for saying no and accepting an escalation to the management sponsor or ask the sponsor to act as the arbiter who settles the dispute, as I discuss in the chapter *Conflict*. Whatever you do, refrain from attacking Sophie or her position. Don't retaliate if you feel treated unfairly, as this will only make things worse. Therefore, be firm on moving towards your main need, but be kind in your speech and actions.

Make Negotiation the Exception, Not the Norm

While you should be able to negotiate, you may choose not to do so. In the example where Sophie demands that a feature is added to the current release, you may choose to negotiate with her along the lines discussed earlier. However, that's not your only option. Instead of entering into a negotiation with Sophie, you could acknowledge her request but ask her to follow the standard process to discuss requests and invite her to the appropriate meeting.[71] Why should you make an exception for her and possibly set a precedent? If the feature must be discussed urgently, then offer to schedule the meeting as soon as possible. Invite the stakeholders and development team and collaboratively decide how to best address Sophie's request. This creates transparency and avoids negotiating a deal with Sophie that you then have to sell to the stakeholders and dev team. Whatever strategy you choose, bear in mind that it is not your job to please stakeholders like Sophie but to create value for the users and business.

If you find that you regularly negotiate, then ask yourself why that is. Here some common causes:

---

71 You may want to discuss new features in a product strategy or sprint review meeting, depending on their impact. You may also want to involve the development team members and stakeholders to benefit from their perspectives and to secure their buy-in. Please see the chapter *Interactions* for more discussion on how to collaborate with the key stakeholders and dev team members.

- You might lack the necessary authority to say no to powerful individuals and enforce joint decisions.
- People might not buy into the vision and product strategy but pursue their own, individual goals. You therefore lack shared overall goals that provide direction and alignment, as discussed in the chapter *Goals*.
- You might not involve the right people in the decision-making process, or you use the wrong decision rule—for example, *product person decides after discussion* instead of *consent* or *unanimous agreement*.
- The individuals are not willing to embrace a collaborative and transparent way of working but try to request or demand special favours from you.

Whatever it may be, I recommend that you stop and reflect on what is really going on and how you can address the underlying cause rather than accepting negotiation as the norm.

SELF-LEADERSHIP

Knowing others is intelligence; knowing yourself is true wisdom.
Mastering others is strength; mastering yourself is true power.
Lao Tzu

The previous chapters of this book focused on practices that help you support and influence others. But without being aware of your own thoughts, emotions, and needs, and without reflecting on your intentions and actions, you will find it challenging to effectively guide the development team and stakeholders. This is where self-leadership comes in. As its name suggests, self-leadership is about developing yourself, about becoming a happier individual and a better leader. But self-leadership and personal growth don't happen by accident. They require the willingness to accept one's shortcomings, make the effort to let go of unskilful habits, and strengthen your positive qualities.

Practise Mindfulness

As product people, we have a demanding job with a diverse range of responsibilities; different tasks compete for our attention. These include reviewing the latest key performance indicators (KPIs), carrying out competitor research, adjusting the product roadmap, updating the product backlog, refining user stories, answering questions from the development team, and addressing urgent support issues. This can cause us to rush from one meeting to the next, work several things at once, and get lost in the busyness of our work. Unfortunately, this approach is not only unproductive but also affects our well-being and reduces our ability to effectively lead others. If you are stressed but not aware of it, it will be hard to stay calm and respond with empathy when a senior stakeholder demands a new feature or your boss harshly criticises the current product performance. Being mindful and leading with presence offers a different path: developing a heightened awareness of what we do and how we do it.

Mindfulness in a Nutshell

Mindfulness means paying attention to the present moment, to what is happening right now. It helps you become more aware of your feelings, thoughts, and moods. Are you feeling calm, relaxed, and content right now? Or are you getting tired of or bored with reading this book? Are you feeling uneasy, tense, restless, or indifferent?

Understanding how we are is important, as our mental state influences how we perceive reality. Here is a simple example from my life: One of my favourite pastime activities is playing the tenor saxophone. Like many other musicians, I practise scales like C major on a daily basis. This routine exercise teaches me important musical skills and improves my control of the instrument. I find that when I am content and relaxed, the scales flow easily and evenly. When I make a mistake, I am able to accept it as part of the learning process. But when I am tense, stressed, or grumpy, my fingers grip the keys harder than necessary, and my embouchure—the way my mouth connects to the mouthpiece—is too tight. Playing the scales feels less pleasant and more like a chore. When I make a mistake, I get self-critical and doubtful. I question my ability to get better at playing the instrument and sometimes even wonder if I should give it up.

When I am not mindful, not aware of my mental state, I get lost in the experience. When things go wrong, I can feel helpless and overwhelmed by frustration and anger, by wanting to achieve but not being able to. When I am mindful, however, I catch myself getting tense and frustrated. This recognition is often enough to soften and relax, not get carried away by unhelpful feelings or thoughts, and relate to the experience in a healthy way. This allows me to see, for example, that I am tired and exhausted after a hard day at work and that this makes playing the saxophone more challenging.

Mindfulness, therefore, is not about suppressing or getting rid of thoughts and feelings, particularly unpleasant ones like envy, anger, fear, or doubt. It is not about reaching blissful or special mental states, judging or fixing things, or being super productive and amazingly successful. It simply means paying attention to what's happing in our inner world so that we become more aware of our feelings and thoughts. This does not mean that we have to like or approve the thoughts and emotions we are experiencing. I certainly don't like it when I feel worry or anger, for instance. But experiencing these feelings is part of human life—just as much as joy, gratitude, or equanimity. We all feel anger sometimes and joy at other times. The point is not to get carried away by our feelings and thoughts, not to take them personally, identify with them, and mistake them for objective reality, but to relate to them wisely. This prevents us from acting out unskilful mental states, saying something we will regret later, or making wrong decisions.

It also invites us to investigate the causes of unpleasant emotions like anger and frustration. If I feel repeatedly angry or frustrated when playing the scales, to stay with the example, then it would be a good idea to ask myself why that is. Am I too ambitious? Do I expect too much of myself? Have I set unrealistic goals? Do I approach the practice in the wrong way? And why is it important to me that I am good at playing the saxophone? What does this tell me about myself, my self-view, and my values and priorities in life?

Benefits of Developing Mindfulness

While mindfulness provides a number of general work-related benefits like improved creativity and productivity, it also offers some specific leadership-related gains for product people, as I describe next.

Greater Serenity

Faced with a demanding job with a diverse range of duties, mindfulness helps you know yourself better and see more clearly how you are. This enables you to catch yourself getting tense and to stop yourself from getting stressed out. With sustained practice, you are more likely to stay calm and collected even in challenging situations. Being serene and calm makes you more trustworthy and pleasant to work with, and it increases the chances that people will follow your lead.

Increased Empathy

As pointed out in the chapter *Introduction*, developing empathy for the users, development team members, and stakeholders is a major success factor for product people. If you do not understand the user needs, then you will struggle to offer a product that does a great job and becomes successful. And if you don't empathise with the stakeholders, people are unlikely to trust and follow you. Luckily, mindfulness practice strengthens your capacity to empathise with others and to be kind and accepting towards yourself. It teaches you to be open-minded and non-judgemental, to observe without evaluating or criticising—qualities that I have found very helpful when interacting with people.

Better Decision-Making

Mindfulness helps you make better decisions for the following two reasons: First, it helps you recognise cognitive biases. These include confirmation bias, the tendency to prefer data that confirm preconceived views; negativity bias, focusing on negative experiences; and overconfidence bias, overestimating the reliability of one's own judgements, control, and chances of success. Recognising these biases reduces the risk of making wrong product decisions—for instance, disregarding valid data because it does not match your view. Second, mindfulness helps you to be more aware of your feelings—for example, how excited, sceptical, or displeased you are. This makes it less likely that your emotions drive a product decision—for example, that being angry with someone prevents you from paying attention to the person's valid concerns.

Improved Communication

Practicing mindfulness makes you less prone to be gripped by emotions, act on impulses, and say something you'll later regret. I find that mindfulness allows me to catch myself getting emotional, upset, or angry. This gives me a choice: I can decide not to immediately respond and wait until I feel calm again, or I can carefully choose my words rather than hearing them streaming out of me, seemingly of their own accord. Being able to speak and write in a wise, reflective fashion increases the clarity of your communication, reduces the likelihood of using words that might upset or hurt people, and gains you the trust and respect of the people you want to lead. What's more, strengthening your capacity to be mindful helps you get better at attentively listening to other people. It makes it easier to recognise when your mind is starting to wander or when you are judging what the other person is saying rather than being receptive and listening with an open mind.[72]

Hold Personal Retrospectives

While we all have the capacity to be mindful, developing a heightened self-awareness doesn't happen without making a dedicated effort. A great way to step away from your work routine and reflect on how

---

72 The practice *Listen Inwardly,* which I discuss in the chapter *Conversations,* is an example of mindfulness applied to communication: It encourages you to pay attention to your thoughts and feelings when listening to others.

you are is to schedule a personal retrospective. Allocate thirty minutes in your calendar towards the end of each work week and ask yourself the following questions:

- What did I get done this week? Which challenges and difficulties did I encounter? What did I learn?
- How am I feeling right now? How did my moods and energy levels develop during the week?
- What changes do I want to make next week?

For example, you might have had a busy, hectic week in which you made important product decisions or launched a major product update. Consequently, you might feel tired but contented. Alternatively, your week might have been challenging, full of difficult conversations and conflict. As a result, you might be exhausted and looking forward to the weekend. In whatever way the week unfolded, honestly reflect on what happened, how you felt, and what you can learn from it. Pay attention to recurring experiences and patterns. For example, have you often been tired and stressed in recent weeks? Do you regularly feel dissatisfied or frustrated? And if that's the case, what are the causes?

When you reflect on any changes you want to make, focus on changing your own attitude and behaviour. Don't be overambitious and try to change too many things at the same time. Rather, select one or two items that you can realistically improve. For instance, if you spoke harshly and lost your patience several times this week, then consider improving either your speaking habits or your patience. Working on both at the same time might be overwhelming and not lead to any sustained improvements in your behaviour.

Write a Journal

In order to keep track of how your well-being evolves and to be able to spot patterns, consider writing a journal. You might want to take a few minutes at the end of each working day to describe how the day went for you, or you might want to capture the outcome of your personal retrospective in the journal. You might even want to jot down what you did and how much time you spend on major tasks. This can help you understand if you are neglecting strategic or tactical duties, for example.

While writing a journal might sound like a big commitment, it will help you process your experiences and derive the right learnings from them. Writing down my feelings and thoughts helps me redefine my relationship to them: I am less caught up in them and can consequently look at them more objectively. This makes it easier to draw the right conclusions and decide what to do. If you are not sure if writing a journal is right for you, then try it out for a couple of weeks. You might find it more beneficial and less work than you imagined.

Meditate

Before I started to meditate, I used to think that meditation was about having an empty mind, not thinking about anything, and feeling nice, pleasant, and relaxed. While meditation can be pleasant and enjoyable, it's certainly not about escaping from reality. The opposite is true: Meditation is a vehicle to experience things for what they are, become more aware of your thoughts and emotions, and get to know yourself better. And knowing yourself better helps you understand and effectively guide others.

You can think of meditation as formal mindfulness practice. A common meditation technique is to patiently and gently observe the breath. This provides you with focus and helps you notice the thoughts and feelings that come up and take your attention away from the breath. But don't expect to achieve or gain anything while meditating, like becoming calm and relaxed. Don't feel bad if your mind wanders or if you experience restlessness; don't ignore or suppress any thoughts and feelings, particularly those that you don't like, such as worries, doubt, fear, anger, and envy. At the same time, try not to latch on to them, solve a problem, or get caught up in thinking about the future or past. If this happens, gently notice it and bring your attention back to the breath.

As mentioned before, the point of mindfulness practice is to help you develop a healthier relationship with your thoughts and feelings, not to suppress them or get rid of them. Therefore, don't be hard on yourself. Instead, cultivate an open, receptive, and curious attitude. Gently and kindly observe how you are, what is happening in your inner world. I find that my mind usually settles and becomes calmer after a few minutes of meditation; difficult thoughts and emotions tend to weaken and often disappear when I acknowledge but don't engage in them.

To maximise its benefits, meditation should be done regularly. Like any exercise, regular short meditation sessions tend to be better than occasional long ones. To sustain your meditation practice, make it part of your daily routine. Meditate in the morning, at lunchtime, and/or in the evening, depending on what suits you best. Start with five or ten minutes and see how that works for you. Over time, you might want to extend the meditation duration to twenty or thirty minutes. Most people sit when they meditate, often on the ground. But you can also use a chair or practise standing and walking meditation. You might even experiment with lying down while meditating.[73]

The One-Minute Meditation

Meditation doesn't necessarily have to be long. A great way to integrate meditation into your daily routine is to have regular shorter meditation sessions. You can even practise one-minute meditations, which unsurprisingly last sixty seconds.[74] To do so, set your timer or meditation app. Close your eyes and settle into your seat. Feel where your bottom is touching the chair or cushion. Become aware of where there is tension in your body—for example, your forehead, neck, or fingers—and relax into the sensation. Pay attention to your breathing. When your mind wanders, when thoughts and feelings arise, then simply notice them. Gently bring your attention back to the breath. When the minute is over, slowly open your eyes. Despite its brevity, the meditation offers you the opportunity to pause and relax, connect with your body and feelings, and become aware of how you are right now.

---

73   The four traditional Buddhist meditation postures are sitting, standing, walking, and lying down.

74   I would like to thank Bhante Sukhacitto for introducing the technique to me.

Embrace a Growth Mindset

"Leadership and learning are indispensable to each other," as John F. Kennedy once noted. In order to be an effective leader, it is important to develop relevant skills, like effectively making decisions and resolving conflict, and to grow as an individual—learn to better deal with difficult mind states and become a more empathic person. Embracing a growth mindset helps you with this.

What Is a Growth Mindset?

Learning something new requires the right attitude. If you believe that you lack talent or are not smart enough, then it will be hard—if not impossible—to acquire new knowledge and skills, as the following story shows. I was about twelve years old when I baked my first cake. The cake was more like a brick than something eatable, and my parents' kitchen was a mess. What a disaster. This experience put me off baking; I had no desire to try it again. Worse, I started to believe that I genuinely was no good at baking. I held on to this belief for decades, and it wasn't until much later in my life that I tried to bake again, inspired by the example of my oldest son. And while I haven't become a master baker yet, my cakes are certainly eatable these days, and I truly enjoy making them.

In addition to embracing a can-do attitude, achievement requires effort and discipline. The better we want to become at something, the more effort we have to invest. I remember once saying to my saxophone teacher that I'd never be as good as him. He looked at me and said, "You will be, once you've started practicing eight hours per day." Charlie Parker, one of the most famous and arguably the best saxophonists ever, took this further and practised up to fifteen hours per day. The difference between being good and being great at something is therefore significantly influenced by how industrious we are.

I am not suggesting that innate talent doesn't exist, but I believe that its role is often overemphasised. This leads to a fixed mindset, where people see themselves as good or bad at something—be it writing, singing, drawing, math, or baking—and they believe that there is not much they can do about it. But the opposite is true: A "person's true potential is unknown (and unknowable)," and "it's impossible to foresee what can be accomplished with years of passion, toil, and training," as Carol Dweck—who coined the term *growth mindset*—writes (Dweck 2017, 7). Instead of labelling yourself as talented, smart, or clever (or possibly the opposite), see yourself as malleable and adaptable. With the right effort, you will learn new skills and deepen existing ones; you will develop and grow. By doing so, you adopt a growth mindset.

Leverage Failure

Learning a new skill can be fun and easy. But it can also be very challenging. Often, it involves stepping outside your comfort zone and making mistakes. Think of what it was like to learn to ride a bicycle, for example. I remember crashing numerous times until I was able to stay upright on the bike, riding wobbly and tentatively at first and then slowly getting better over time.

The same is true for product management. For instance, when you lead a product for the first time, you are likely to make mistakes. You might not involve the development team members and stakeholders enough in important decisions, or you might try to please everyone and end up with weak compromises. Similarly, when you create a product strategy for the first time, your target group may end up being too big and heterogeneous, the value proposition may not be concise and compelling enough, the standout features of your product may not be terribly exciting, or the business goals may not be measurable. But that's OK—as long as you recognise the mistakes and are willing to learn from them.

Therefore, don't let failure discourage you. See it as a necessary part of the learning journey rather than something bad that should be avoided. Be patient, don't put yourself under pressure, don't try to force success, and don't beat yourself up if you don't succeed. I can be very self-critical and have thoughts like *I am no good at this* and *I'll never get it* when I make a mistake. While it's normal to have doubts, acting on those thoughts would be giving in to a fixed mindset. Instead, practise self-compassion, reflect on your learning approach, persevere, and have faith in your ability to develop and grow. With the right effort, you will get better. It might just take a little while.

Foster an Open Mind

Believing in our ability to learn and grow sounds like common sense. So why don't we always show a growth mindset? An important reason is our attachment to what we know and who we think we are. Whether we are aware of it or not, we tend to be fond of the knowledge and skills that we have acquired; the more we know, the more expertise we have on a given subject and the more attached and less open to new insights and change we usually are. If you've successfully done strategy work for your product across different life-cycle stages, for example, then you are likely to be convinced that your approach, your way of working, is right. If a colleague uses new or different techniques, then it is easy to dismiss them. You know what works best for your product, after all. But do you?

To take full advantage of a growth mindset, cultivate an open mind, a receptive and curious attitude. To do so, hold your knowledge, views, and beliefs lightly. Realise that learning something new often requires letting go of existing ideas, knowledge, and behaviour. What's more, views are relative, and there is no one right way. People have different preferences and needs, and different circumstances call for different approaches. What worked well for a development team in the past may not be the best approach for another team. Don't identify with your knowledge and beliefs, and don't let them define who you are. Otherwise they will hold you back, and you won't be able to fulfil your true potential.

Developing an open mind provides you with an inner agility. It makes it easier to leverage mistakes and to learn from difficult feedback, as you are less concerned with being right; it counteracts mental biases like the tendency to look for data that confirm your views (confirmation bias); and it facilitates effective collaboration: With an open mind, you will be more receptive and able to appreciate other people's ideas and perspectives.

Learn Something New

A great way to cultivate a growth mindset is to learn a new skill—for example, draw or paint, sing, play an instrument, take up yoga, learn a new language, or learn to program. For example, I have benefitted a lot from (re)learning to play the saxophone—after not having played it for more than twenty years. I have learnt not only about playing a wind instrument and music in general but also, and more importantly, about myself, including how driven and impatient I can be. It has helped me see how valuable failure is in order to progress: It's impossible to get better at playing an instrument without stepping out of your comfort zone, challenging yourself, and making mistakes. But I have also learnt to be more patient and not wanting to achieve too much too quickly.

An alternative way to counteract a fixed mindset is to collaborate with others. For instance, invite a colleague to one of your strategy workshops or sprint review meetings, or prioritise the product backlog together. This will challenge some of your views and beliefs, help you reflect on your own practice, and offer the opportunity to pick up new ideas and techniques. It is also a great opportunity to learn something about yourself. Are you, for example, critical of the other person's work and quick to exercise judgement? Are you pleased for the individual or envious when a colleague is better at something? Finally, practicing mindfulness—as I suggested earlier—will allow you see to more clearly what you hold dearly and what you are attached to. It will help you better understand your defaults, tendencies, and preferences and develop an open, receptive, and curious mind.

Cultivate Self-Compassion

We can be so driven by trying to achieve goals, proving ourselves, and supporting others that we forget to take good care of ourselves. I know a number of people who have suffered from heart attacks, lasting food intolerances, and prolapses due to the stress levels they experienced while working on digital products. One person even committed suicide. While these cases are extreme, they show what can happen when you continuously sacrifice your own well-being. Additionally, many of us, including myself, have high expectations of ourselves and can be very self-critical. While becoming aware of your weaknesses is helpful to develop and grow, beating yourself up and feeling bad or guilty does not benefit anyone.

Self-compassion counteracts these tendencies. It "involves wanting health and well-being for oneself," as Neff (2015, 12) puts it. This does not imply that you regard your needs as more important than others and act in selfish ways. It means being kind towards yourself, without ignoring the shortcomings you might have. Imagine that in the last product backlog refinement session, you lost patience with Josh, one of the development team members, and you spoke harshly to him. Consequently, Josh felt hurt, stopped participating in the workshop, and went to his phone for the remainder of the session. You are now on your way home from work. The event is playing on your mind, and you are feeling bad and guilty. You might think, *How could I speak so harshly to Josh and call him dumb? I'm a poor leader. I'll never learn to constructively deal with my feelings and say the right things.*

Now, honest reflection and the willingness to recognise one's shortcomings—having harshly spoken to Josh—are helpful, as they are the prerequisites for learning and growth. But being overly self-critical and self-judgemental—being a poor leader and never learning to say the right thing—does not help. It reinforces the feeling of not being good enough. This can lead to low self-esteem and to feeling miserable and depressed. If you find it hard to forgive yourself, bring to mind that, as human beings, we all make mistakes; we have said or done something that wasn't skilful. Additionally, promise yourself to talk to Josh as soon as possible and apologise for your behaviour.

If you find it hard to let go of overly self-critical thoughts, remind yourself of your strengths and positive qualities. Think about all the good things you have done and the kindness you have shown to people. Finally, reflect on your self-view, the expectations you put on yourself, and who you think you should or want to be. I find that the higher the expectations I have of myself, the more I put myself under pressure, and the more likely I am to be disappointed. Now, I am not suggesting you should not have any goals or ideas about how you can better yourself. But set realistic goals, and don't be too hard on yourself if you fail to make enough progress. Old habits die hard: It takes time to change ingrained behaviour patterns and views that we have held for a long time.

Carefully Manage Your Time

As product people, we usually have a demanding job that often seems to require more time than we have. It is therefore important that you are aware of your workload and carefully manage your time. The following practices will help you with this.

Adopt a Sustainable Pace

Sustainable pace is an important agile principle. The "*Manifesto for Agile Software Development*" defines it in the following way: "The sponsors, developers, and users should be able to maintain a constant pace indefinitely" (Beck et. al. 2001). The goal is to create a healthy work environment and to avoid that people are routinely overworked, lose their creativity, make mistakes, and eventually sacrifice their health. A framework like Scrum offers specific techniques that ensure sustainable pace—unfortunately, only for development team members.[75]

But sustainable pace is equally important for you, the person in charge of the product. With different duties competing for your time and attention, it is all too easy to do too much, work too hard. But rushing from one task to the next and from one meeting to another is counter-productive: When I am in a rush, I am likely to make mistakes. What's more, I get tense, restless, and stressed. This reduces my attention span and, over time, negatively impacts my sleep. In the worst case, I am trapped in a downward spiral, getting more and more irritable and finding it increasingly hard to stay focused, attentively listen to others, and keep up with the demands at work.

In order to avoid being overworked, don't cram too much into your day. If you feel that there is more work to do than you can realistically accomplish, then ruthlessly prioritise and learn to say no, as I discuss next. Focus on the most important tasks; delegate or postpone others. For instance, the development team may be able to refine some user stories without you, or the sales team may not require a separate update on the new release, if you encourage the individuals to attend the next sprint review meeting.

A simple trick that stops me from rushing around is to walk slowly, as you would when you go for a nice, leisurely walk. Here is one example of how this has helped me: I used to walk as quickly as possible from the airplane to the passport control at Heathrow Airport every time I was coming home from a business trip, until I finally realised that this saved me a couple of minutes but made me stressed. I consequently started to pay attention to my walking and to slow down my pace even if others overtake me. I now feel more relaxed when I leave the airport and less tense when I arrive at home.

---

75 This includes giving the development team the authority to decide how much work can be taken on for a given sprint. The team essentially determines the workload.

Additionally, many people have a specific time when they are most creative and productive. Mine is in the morning; I tend to be most creative between 8:00 and 11:00 a.m., and hence I tend to block that time for demanding work. Whatever your creative time of the day is, try to use it for mentally demanding tasks—for example, competitor analysis or strategy reviews. This will help you increase your productivity without sacrificing sustainable pace.

Do One Thing at a Time

It can be tempting to task switch and jump from one task to the next to get more work done. But in reality, it reduces our productivity. Every time we start a new task, be it reading an email, talking to a colleague, or looking at new analytics data, we need time to remind ourselves what has to be done and how to do it. This quickly adds up, particularly when we frequently task switch. What's more, I find that working on several things at once is tiring. It can lead to restlessness, which makes it hard to relax after work. Therefore, do one thing at a time, and don't multitask. Be present and fully engaged in what you do—or don't do it. A thing worth doing is worth doing well, as the old saying goes.

To focus your efforts, consider setting yourself a daily goal. Spend a few minutes in the morning planning your day, and decide what the main thing is that you want to achieve and what the desired outcome should be. Take into account any commitments in your calendar to ensure that your goal is realistic. This technique helps me direct my work; it prevents me from being reactive and jumping from one task to the next, depending on what seems to be most urgent, and it provides me with a sense of satisfaction: When I look back at the day in the evening, I know I have done something meaningful—worked towards my goal and hopefully achieved it—in addition to smaller, urgent tasks that had to be tackled.

Don't Neglect the Important but Less Urgent Work

As your time is precious, it can be helpful to reflect on what type of work you do—where you spend your time. One way to do this is to categorise the various tasks according to their urgency and importance, a technique originally created by Dwight D. Eisenhower. This creates a matrix with four quadrants, as figure 5 shows.

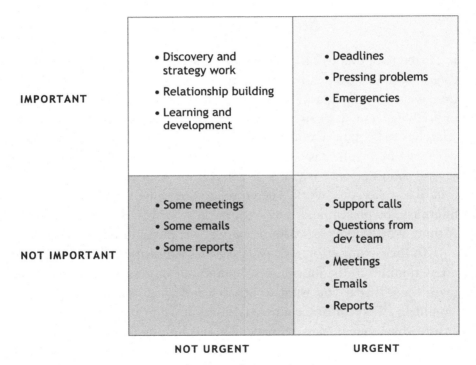

Figure 5: *Eisenhower Matrix*[76]

As figure 5 illustrates, there are urgent and important tasks, such as deadlines and critical problems. Next, there are urgent but less important activities, such as answering questions from the dev team, attending meetings, and answering emails. Then there are less urgent

---

76   The matrix is based on Covey (2013, 160).

but important tasks, like carrying out product discovery and strategy work, building relationships with stakeholders and customers, and acquiring new skills. Finally, some activities are neither very important nor urgent; think of some of the meetings you might attend or emails you read.

I find that some product people attend so much to the urgent work that the less pressing but important tasks, including product discovery and strategy work, don't receive the necessary attention. This is problematic because it is likely to create more urgent work in the future: If you don't regularly review the product performance and watch out for new trends and competitors, then you may get caught out and experience nasty surprises in the future. For example, a competitor might leapfrog you, or your product may no longer be properly differentiated. Therefore, make time for the less urgent but important tasks—at least half a day, as a rule of thumb. Ring-fence this time, and do not sacrifice it for urgent tasks.

If you find that there is so much pressing work to do, try the following three strategies: First, stop doing less important tasks, or delegate them, something I recommended earlier. Do you really need to attend all meetings you currently participate in? Do you need to receive and read all emails that are sent to you? Can you get off some distribution lists, or can someone else take care of the messages? Second, timebox routine work. For instance, check and answer messages for thirty minutes in the morning, after lunch, and towards the end of the day. Set a timer and stop the activity when the time is up, then close your email or social media app and disable notifications. This allows you to better understand how much time you spend on the various tasks, and it increases your productivity and mental well-being: The less task switching you do and the fewer interruptions you have, the more you will get done and the less restless and stressed you will tend to be. Third, review your recurring tasks: Do they help you manage the product and lead the dev team and stakeholders? If not, why are you carrying out the tasks? As discussed in the chapter *Interactions*, it's a mistake to take on additional responsibilities and to cover other people's work on a continued basis. If you have started, for example, to perform some Scrum Master work, like process coaching or impediments removal, then focus on your actual job and stop taking on other people's work. Be willing to set boundaries, say no, and let go: You can't do everything without either neglecting your core responsibilities or sacrificing your health, neither of which is desirable.

Take Regular Breaks

It can be tempting to keep busy: Getting things done can be exciting and rewarding, and being busy can make us feel useful and wanted. But if we are always "on," if we work through our lunchtime and check work emails in the evening, for instance, then we are not able to recover and recharge our batteries. We are stuck in a work bubble and in danger of running out of energy and creativity. I find it impossible to come up with new ideas and to be creative when I am overworked and tired.

Therefore, make sure that you take regular breaks from work. Have proper lunchtime breaks and get away from your desk, at least from time to time. Go for a walk, do some exercise, or chat with colleagues—but try not to talk about work. Don't check your phone in the evening unless there is an emergency. When you are on holiday, try to let go of work-related thoughts. Don't read work emails, don't take calls from the office, and don't read books that are related to your work. Let go, unwind, recharge, and get a fresh perspective on things.

Work may be important, but don't allow it to take over your life and define who you are. At some point in time, your job will change or end: Your product might get retired, or you will retire.

There is more to life than work.

ACKNOWLEDGEMENTS

A book is never the achievement of a single person. As authors, we are indebted to the people on whose ideas we've drawn and to the individuals who have supported us in writing the book. I want to first and foremost thank my wife, Melissa Pichler, who was invaluable in discussing ideas and generating new ones and who patiently reviewed draft chapters of this book, even as I kept reworking them. Without her input, this book would not be what it is. Thank you, honey! I'd also like to wholeheartedly thank Marc Abraham, Kerry Golding, Stefan Roock, and Jim Siddle for taking the time to review the book and offering valuable feedback. Thanks to Marc Abraham, Mike Cohn, and Cindy Turrietta for helping me choose the book title, which always seems to be a challenge for me. And last but not least, I'd like to thank my parents, for showing me that there is more to life than money and success, and my spiritual teachers, particularly at Amaravati Monastery in Hertfordshire, United Kingdom, for offering guidance on becoming a happier, freer person.

ABOUT THE AUTHOR

Roman Pichler works as a product management consultant, teacher, and writer. He has a long track record of teaching and mentoring product managers, advising product leaders, and helping companies create successful product management organisations. He is the author of three other books, including *Agile Product Management with Scrum* and *Strategize: Product Strategy and Product Roadmap Practices for the Digital Age*, and he writes a popular product management blog. As the founder and director of Pichler Consulting, Roman looks after the company's products and services. This keeps his product management practice fresh, and it allows him to experiment with new ideas. Roman lives with his wife and three children near London, United Kingdom. You can contact Roman at info@romanpichler.com, and you can find out more about his work at www.romanpichler.com.

REFERENCES

Ackermann, Fran, and Colin Eden. *Making Strategy: Mapping Out Strategic Success*. 2nd ed. Los Angeles: SAGE, 2011.

Amro, Ajahn. "Negative States of Mind." Amaravati. September 24, 2018. www.amaravati.org/audio/negative-states-of-mind.

Avery, Christopher. *The Responsibility Process: Unlocking Your Natural Ability to Live and Lead with Power*. Pflugerville, TX: Partnerwerks, 2016. Kindle.

Beck, Kent, Mike Beedle, Arie van Bennekum, Alistair Cockburn, Ward Cunningham, Martin Fowler, James Grenning, et al. "Manifesto for Agile Software Development." 2001. www.agilemanifesto.org.

Blank, Steve. "Ardent 2: Get Out of My Building." October 8, 2009. steveblank.com/2009/10/08/get-out-of-my-building.

Brown, Tim. *Change by Design: How Design Thinking Transforms Organizations and Inspires Innovation*. New York: HarperCollins, 2009.

Buck, John A., and Sharon Villines. *We the People: Consenting to a Deeper Democracy*. 2nd ed. Washington, DC: Sociocracy.info Press, 2017. Kindle.

Cain, Áine. "Steve Jobs and Jeff Bezos' mentor used a simple test to figure out who is a true leader." October 14, 2017. www.businessinsider.com.au/silicon-valley-coach-bill-campbell-leadership-2017-10.

Case, Amber. *Calm Technology: Designing for Billions of Devices and the Internet of Things*. Boston: O'Reilly Media, 2015.

Cialdini, Robert B. *Influence: The Psychology of Persuasion*. Rev. ed. New York: HarperCollins, 2009.

Cohen, Andrea S., Susan Partnow, and Leah Green. *Practicing the Art of Compassionate Listening*. 2nd ed. Indianola, WA: The Compassionate Listening Project, 2017.

Covey, Stephen R. *The 7 Habits of Highly Effective People: Powerful Lessons in Personal Change*. New York: RosettaBooks, 2013. Kindle.

de Bono, Edward. *Six Thinking Hats*. New York: Penguin Life, 2016.

Dweck, Carol. *Mindset: Changing the Way You Think to Fulfil Your Potential*. 6th ed. London: Robinson, 2017. Kindle.

Fisher, Roger, and William Ury. *Getting to Yes: Negotiating Agreement without Giving In*. London: Cornerstone Digital, 2012.

Goleman, Daniel, Richard Boyatzis, and Annie McKee. *Primal Leadership: Unleashing the Power of Emotional Intelligence*. Boston: Harvard Business School Publishing, 2013.

Greenleaf, Robert K. *Servant Leadership: A Journey into the Nature of Legitimate Power and Greatness*. 25th ann. ed. Mahwah, NJ: Paulist Press, 2002.

Hackman, J. Richard. *Collaborative Intelligence: Using Teams to Solve Hard Problems*. San Francisco: Berrett-Koehler, 2011. Kindle.

Hartnett, Tim. *Consensus-Oriented Decision-Making*. Gabriola Island, Canada: New Society Publishers, 2010.

Kaner, Sam, Lenny Lind, Catherine Toldi, Sarah Fisk, and Duane Berger. *Facilitator's Guide to Participatory Decision-Making*. 3rd ed. San Francisco: Jossey-Bass, 2014.

Lafley, A. G., and Roger L. Martin. *Playing to Win: How Strategy Really Works*. Boston: Harvard Business School Publishing, 2013.

Lencioni, Patrick. *The Five Dysfunctions of a Team: A Leadership Fable*. San Francisco: Jossey-Bass, 2002.

Mamoli, Sandy, and David Mole. *Creating Great Teams: How Self-Selection Lets People Excel*. Raleigh, NC: Pragmatic Bookshelf, 2015.

Neff, Kristin. *Self-Compassion: The Proven Power of Being Kind to Yourself*. New York: William Morrow, 2015. Kindle.

Pichler, Roman. *Agile Product Management with Scrum: Creating Products that Customers Love*. Upper Saddle River, NJ: Addison-Wesley, 2010.

———. "Scaling the Product Owner Role." June 28, 2016. www.romanpichler.com/blog/scaling-the-product-owner.

———. *Strategize: Product Strategy and Product Roadmap Practices for the Digital Age*. Wendover, United Kingdom: Pichler Consulting Limited, 2016.

———. "The T-Shaped Product Manager." May 10, 2017. www.romanpichler.com/blog/the-t-shaped-product-manager.

Rosenberg, Marshall B. *Nonviolent Communication: A Language of Life*. 3rd ed. Encinitas, CA: PuddleDancer Press, 2015. Kindle.

Rowe, Ben. "The Rise of the Ethical Product Designer." December 23, 2018. www.uxmas.com/2018/the-rise-of-design-ethics.

Sitkin, Sim B., Chet Miller, and Kelly E. See. "The Stretch Goal Paradox." *Harvard Business Review* (2017, January–February): 92–99.

Smith, Preston G., and Donald G. Reinertsen. *Developing Products in Half the Time: New Rules, New Tools*. 2nd ed. New York: Wiley, 1998.

Sofer, Oren Jay. *Say What You Mean: A Mindful Approach to Nonviolent Communication*. Boulder, CO: Shambhala, 2018. Kindle.

Sosik, John J., and Dongil Jung. *Full Range Leadership Development: Pathways for People, Profit, and Planet*. New York: Psychology Press, 2011. Kindle.

Stavros, Jackie, and Cheri Torres. *Conversations Worth Having: Using Appreciative Inquiry to Fuel Productive and Meaningful Engagement*. Oakland, CA: Berrett-Koehler, 2018. Kindle.

Stone, Douglas, Bruce Patton, and Sheila Heen. *Difficult Conversations: How to Discuss What Matters Most*. 10th ann. ed. New York: Penguin Books, 2010.

Surowiecki, James. *The Wisdom of Crowds: Why the Many Are Smarter Than the Few.* London: Abacus, 2004.

Thanissaro, Bhikkhu. "Right Speech: Samma Vaca." November 30, 2013. www.accesstoinsight.org/ptf/dhamma/sacca/sacca4/samma-vaca/index.html.

Tuckman, Bruce. "Developmental Sequence in Small Groups." *Psychological Bulletin* 63 (1965): 384–99.

Voss, Chris. *Never Split the Difference: Negotiating as if Your Life Depended on It.* New York: HarperBusiness, 2016. Kindle.

INDEX

A

Accountability 44
  Being accountable for reaching agreed
    goals 15, 30, 32, 54
Achievement 53, 55, 148, 159
Agreement 119, 162
  Scale 119
Alignment 52
Anger 74, 79, 80, 91-93, 98, 99, 102, 103,
    108, 133, 142, 146
Artificial harmony 18, 86, 93, 94, 128
Attention 14, 34, 59, 63-67, 70, 82, 84, 92,
    102, 104, 115, 123, 134, 140-142,
    144-147, 154, 157
Attitude 7, 10, 55, 64, 67, 79, 88, 98-100,
    132, 133, 145, 147, 148, 150
Authority 1, 5, 7, 19, 40, 42, 123, 139, 154
Autonomy 46, 52
Awareness 29, 65, 141, 144

B

Behaviour 8, 12-14, 34, 44, 45, 57, 61, 75,
    78, 79, 86, 87, 91, 93, 94, 96, 99,
    100, 101, 104, 106-108, 118, 132,
    137, 145, 150, 153
  Addictive 57
  Aggressive 86, 87
  Competitive 86
  Inappropriate 44, 45, 75, 93, 100

Behaviour change 106, 107
Behavioural change stairway model 6, 131
Benefit 9, 13, 25, 35, 48-52, 57, 58, 61,
    75, 77, 82, 89, 91, 97, 105, 112,
    116-118, 123, 138, 152
Bias, *see* cognitive bias
Blame 15, 86, 89, 92, 93, 95, 96, 101, 102,
    108, 109, 112, 123
Body language 65-67, 70, 71, 81, 82
Budget 27, 41, 54, 134, 136, 137
Burndown chart
  Release 20
  Sprint 20
Business goal 47, 49, 50, 53
Business strategy 38, 42, 48
Buy-in 37, 58, 69, 73, 113, 119, 123, 138

C

Change 4, 6-8, 11, 14, 19, 20-22, 35, 37,
    47-50, 54, 56, 58, 69, 76-78, 88, 89,
    106-108, 112, 118, 120-122, 129,
    131, 132, 137, 145, 150, 153, 158
Coaching 12, 42, 69, 76, 158
Cognitive bias
  Confirmation bias 63, 91, 111, 143, 151
  Negativity bias 111, 143
  Overconfidence bias 143
Collaboration 17, 19, 25, 34, 39, 40, 41,
    51, 85, 94, 95, 119, 151

Collaborative decision-making 40, 58, 59, 110, 111, 113, 115, 117, 118, 122, 126, 127
Commitment 27, 111, 146
Communication 9, 44, 67, 95, 96, 98, 101, 104-107, 109, 144
Community 38
Compassion 67, 95, 100, 150, 152
Concern 17
Conflict 16, 23, 33, 44, 45, 76, 80, 85-89, 91-96, 98, 99, 101-103, 105, 106, 108, 109, 128, 131, 145, 148
  Resolution 86, 95, 100, 108, 109
Confrontation 86, 87, 88, 94
Consensus 44, 119, 162
Consent 118, 121-123, 125, 130, 139
Context 14, 24, 36, 37, 39, 43, 69, 75
Conversation 23, 44, 45, 60-62, 64-72, 75, 76, 78-80, 82-84, 96, 101, 108, 109, 131, 134, 135
Creativity 7, 21, 27, 39, 42, 55, 69, 85, 95, 111, 119, 143, 154, 158
Criticism 78, 89, 90, 96, 98, 101, 107
Cross-functional 2, 25, 26
Culture 14, 56, 59, 94

D

Daily Scrum 19, 29, 30, 76
Data 4, 34, 57, 75, 89, 90, 97, 101, 105, 112, 114, 129, 130, 143, 144, 151, 155
Decision 4, 18, 22, 27, 40, 44, 45, 52, 56, 58, 59, 69, 70, 73, 79, 111-127, 130, 131, 139, 143, 144, 162
Decision-making 18, 31, 40, 58, 59, 73, 90, 95, 105, 110, 111-123, 126, 127, 130, 131, 139, 143, 162
  Process 19, 126, 161
Decision rule 115, 118-125, 127, 130, 139
Delegation 59, 119, 125
Delegative 12, 14, 15
Democratic 12

Design by committee 120, 127
Desire 9, 70, 81, 84, 88-89, 91, 106, 130, 148
Development team 2-5, 8, 11, 13-17, 19-21, 23, 25, 27-31, 33-35, 41-43, 46, 47, 50-52, 55, 56, 58-63, 74, 76, 86, 91, 109-111, 113, 114, 118, 119, 121-125, 136, 138, 140, 141, 143, 149, 150, 152, 154
Disagree and commit 124
Disagreement 23, 67, 85, 86, 89, 92, 94, 95, 99, 109, 117, 120, 121, 128
Discovery, see product discovery 21, 27, 34, 42, 43, 134, 157
Dispute 100, 102, 105, 107-109, 138
Diversity 111, 117, 128

E

Effort 4, 10, 13, 17, 19, 23, 25, 32, 43, 52-54, 63, 67, 78, 82, 90, 97, 116, 118, 124, 127, 129, 130-134, 137, 140, 144, 148-150
Eisenhower matrix 156
Emotion 97, 103, 104
Empathy 8, 9, 17, 40, 55, 64, 87, 93, 100, 105, 106, 132, 133, 141, 143
Empowerment 114
  Being empowered 31, 56
  Empowering others 20, 27
Ethical product 57, 163
Expectation 28
Expertise 2, 10, 13, 14, 17, 18, 22, 38, 42, 111, 113, 118, 125, 150

F

Facebook 56, 57
Facilitator 113, 115, 117, 124, 162
Facts 68, 74, 101, 117, 124, 129
Failure 18, 53, 54, 130, 149, 151
Fear 7, 28, 74, 92, 94, 99, 102, 103, 142, 146

Feelings 7, 65, 66, 68-70, 79, 80, 84, 85, 91-94, 96, 98, 102-106, 108, 133, 141, 142, 144, 146, 147, 152
Flipping 33, 77, 84 , 107
Forgiveness 98, 100
Framing 33, 77, 107

G

Goal 31, 40, 51, 53, 163
  Inspirational 12
  Measurable 49, 50, 52, 53, 149
  Shared 1, 3, 5, 7, 37, 39, 40, 42, 95
  Visionary 48
Gossip 80
Ground rules 19, 40, 41, 44, 113, 117, 118, 124
Group 1-3, 6, 11, 13, 14, 18, 21, 26, 38-40, 45, 48, 49, 51, 78-80, 84, 85, 109, 111, 115-121, 123, 125, 126, 128, 129, 136, 149
  Cohesion 13, 14
Growth 106, 148
Growth mindset 11, 148-151
Guidance 4, 14, 18, 23, 34, 48, 53, 113, 117, 159

H

Habit 9

I

Impact 4, 14, 24, 31, 35, 45, 47, 55, 57, 58, 70, 76, 77, 81, 88, 95, 104, 109, 110-114, 122-124, 126, 136, 138
Improvement 20, 35, 41
Influence 1, 3, 5, 6, 8, 11, 27, 36, 37, 38, 62, 115, 125, 126, 132, 137, 140, 162
Integrity 17, 83
Intel 94, 124
Intention 8, 9, 10, 64, 67, 72-76, 83, 89, 97

Interest 2, 6-8, 10, 17, 35-38, 45, 67, 80, 92, 105, 106, 108, 113, 124, 128, 130, 132, 134, 135

J

Job 4, 20, 24, 25, 28, 33, 35-37, 42, 50, 53, 76, 77, 81, 106, 136, 138, 140, 143, 153, 158
  Description 28
  Good job, as in being successful 20, 33, 53
Journal 145, 146

K

Kanban 5, 28-30, 43, 51
Key performance indicators 42, 49, 53, 70, 112
Kindness 79, 153
Kind speech 79, 80
KPIs 42, 49, 53, 70, 140

L

Leader 3, 9, 12, 13, 30, 111, 140, 148, 152, 161
Leadership 1, 4, 7-14, 16, 20, 24, 65, 94, 95, 102, 103, 111, 140, 143, 148, 161-163
Leadership style 1, 12, 14, 102
  Affiliative 12, 15
  Autocratic 12, 111
  Coaching 12, 42, 69, 76, 158
  Delegative 12, 14, 15
  Democratic 12
  Directive 12, 13, 15, 83
  Visionary 12, 13, 15, 48, 52
Learning 10, 11, 22, 35, 40, 57, 67, 95, 106, 141, 148-153
Listening 8, 17, 44, 60-66, 68- 72, 78, 83, 95, 101, 108, 111, 123, 132, 135, 144, 162

M

Majority 68, 118, 121, 122
Management 3, 7, 10, 11, 14, 18-22, 25,
   32, 34, 39, 41, 48, 54, 76, 90, 113,
   114, 118, 138, 149, 160, 163
Manager 2, 4, 19, 20, 30, 45, 85, 108,
   131, 163
Measure 53, 85
Mediation 109
Meditation 109 146, 147
Meeting 9, 19, 30, 33, 44, 49, 50, 52,
   54, 55, 58, 61, 66, 76, 82, 84, 92,
   93-95, 97, 98, 105, 109, 114, 115,
   117, 118, 123, 124, 135, 136, 138,
   141, 154
Mindfulness 65, 103, 140-144, 146, 147,
   151
Mindset 11, 93, 98, 108, 113, 115-118,
   123, 131, 134, 137, 148-151, 162
Morale 35, 109
Motivation 27, 48, 70, 111, 112, 129

N

Needs 3, 6-10, 12, 13, 23, 27, 39, 40, 45,
   49, 50, 52, 68, 70, 73, 85, 86, 88,
   92, 94, 96, 99, 101, 104-106, 108,
   111, 113, 114, 116, 123, 126-130,
   132-137, 140, 143, 150, 152
Negative 9, 58, 65, 68, 70, 77, 80, 84, 86,
   88, 98, 99, 103, 106, 111, 132, 133,
   143, 161
No, as *in saying no* 81
Non-violent communication 95-97
NVC 95, 96
   See non-violent communication

O

Objectives and key results, *see* OKRs
OKRs 53
Open mind 17, 43, 45, 59, 63, 67, 88,
   116, 117, 123, 129, 144, 150, 151

Options, in *conflict resolution* and
   negotiation 111, 112, 120, 127,
   130, 131, 132, 136
Organisational change 11, 19, 21
Ownership 4, 24, 27, 28, 41, 42, 44, 52,
   58, 69, 95, 112, 119

P

Patience 59, 71, 135, 145, 152
Pause, in a *conversation*
Performance 3, 14, 26, 32, 42, 49, 53, 55,
   70, 76, 82, 112, 140, 141, 157
Perspective 6, 7, 9, 23, 29, 30, 33, 34, 45,
   54, 65, 80, 89, 90, 99-102, 113,
   116, 128, 132, 133, 158
Persuasion 73, 162
Plan 14, 20, 25, 38, 63, 66, 67, 69, 79
Player, as a key stakeholder
Position, in *negotiation*
Power 1, 2, 36, 37, 38, 68, 101, 104, 110,
   111, 113, 137, 140, 161, 162, 163
Power-interest grid 36, 37, 38, 113
Pressure 31, 54, 55, 59, 73, 79, 99, 104,
   117, 120, 137, 149, 153
Principled negotiation method 131
Priority 9, 31, 32, 94
Process 5, 8, 13, 19-21, 24, 30, 42, 44, 58,
   66, 73, 76, 78, 79, 108, 111, 113-116,
   118-123, 126, 127, 130, 131, 138,
   139, 141, 146, 158
Product backlog 4, 5, 13, 20, 23, 27-29,
   31-33, 47, 51, 84, 86, 94, 114, 124,
   125, 141, 151, 152
Product development 43, 52, 90
Product discovery 42
Product goal 47, 50, 51, 81
Productivity 5, 26, 39, 95, 109, 143, 155,
   157
Product management 90, 160, 163
   Challenges 1
   Expertise 10
   Group 2, 3, 39

Maturity 11, 101
Responsibilities 40
Skills 25, 35
Tasks 32
Product roadmap 3, 4, 8, 13, 14, 18, 21, 42, 50, 67, 69, 76, 79, 80, 86, 91, 94, 97, 113, 118, 121, 135-137, 141
Product strategy 4, 8, 18, 27, 38, 42, 43, 47, 49, 50, 91, 110, 112, 113, 118, 125, 129, 138, 139, 149
Psychological safety 8, 128
Purpose 30, 46

Q

Questions 5, 20, 27, 32, 40, 52, 61, 63, 69, 70, 83, 103, 104, 117, 127, 135, 136, 141, 145, 156
Clarifying questions 69, 83
Open-ended questions 135
Why questions 70

R

Rapport 71, 80, 132, 133, 135
Release 3, 20, 50, 51, 73, 75, 76, 81, 118, 131, 136, 138, 154
Request 9, 43, 44, 45, 73, 75, 76, 81, 82, 97, 106-108, 127, 133-135, 138, 139
Requirements 5, 27, 28, 35, 60
Respect 7, 17, 18, 39, 40, 44, 62, 74, 75, 79, 96, 97, 105, 106, 115-117, 129, 134, 135, 144
Responsibility 14, 20, 28, 29, 30, 40, 54, 57, 59, 93, 102, 106, 108, 109, 161
Retrospective 15, 19, 30, 32-35, 41, 145, 146
Right speech 72, 164

S

Scaling 4, 42, 163
Scrum 5, 11, 16, 17, 19-23, 27-30, 32-34, 41, 43-45, 51, 59, 76, 77, 87, 90, 109, 116, 122, 154, 158, 160, 163

Scrum Master 11, 16, 17, 19-23, 27, 30, 33, 34, 41, 44, 45, 76, 87, 109, 116, 158
Self-compassion 67, 95, 150, 152, 163
Self-organisation 21, 28
Self-selection 24
Servant leadership 9, 162
Shared product leadership 4
Skills 2, 10, 11, 19, 21, 22, 25-27, 34, 35, 68, 76, 109, 116, 141, 148, 149, 150, 157
Sponsor 11, 45, 113, 118, 138
Sprint 3, 5, 13, 15, 19, 20, 25, 27-33, 35, 37, 41, 43, 44, 47, 51-53, 56, 58, 59, 63, 69, 86, 114, 122-125, 138, 151, 154
Sprint goal 13, 15, 29, 30-33, 47, 51-53, 59, 86, 114
Sprint planning 5, 19, 28, 31, 32, 122
Sprint retrospective 15, 19, 30, 32, 35, 41
Sprint review 3, 19, 37, 43, 44, 123, 124, 138, 151, 154
Stakeholder 2, 8, 36, 38-41, 43-45, 73, 75, 79, 109, 113, 141
Stakeholder analysis, *see* power-interest grid
Stakeholder community 38
Stretch goal 55, 56
Success 24, 113, 161
Sustainable pace 31, 153, 154, 155

T

Tactics 4, 52
Team 2-5, 8, 11, 13-35, 41-43, 46, 47, 50, 51, 52, 55, 56, 58-63, 74, 76, 77, 85, 86, 91, 109-111, 113, 114, 117-119, 121-125, 127, 131, 136-138, 140, 141, 143, 149, 150, 152, 154, 156, 157
Agile team 5, 28
Component team 24, 25
Feature team 25
Technique 24, 73, 77, 79, 100, 112, 119, 120, 127, 146, 147, 155, 156
Thought 106

Time management, *see* sustainable pace
Transparency 34, 44, 138
True north 48
Trust 7, 8, 10, 16-18, 23, 26, 28, 38-40,
    56, 60-62, 71, 73-75, 78, 79, 83,
    88, 94-96, 100, 105, 106, 109, 114,
    115, 117, 119, 125, 128, 132-135,
    137, 143, 144
Truth, as in *speaking the truth* 17, 44, 72,
    74, 75, 77, 86, 89, 116

U

Unanimous agreement 121, 139
User 2, 4, 10, 13, 14, 20, 25-28, 30, 33, 41,
    42, 46-50, 53, 56-59, 63, 69, 105,
    114, 122, 125, 131, 141, 143, 154

User experience 27, 33, 41, 69
User goal 49

V

Value proposition 21, 50, 57, 69, 70, 113,
    149
Values 19, 39, 89, 106, 116, 142
Vision 4, 42, 46-49, 52, 53, 56, 58, 59, 139

W

Win-lose 86, 88, 122
Win-win 137
Work environment 5, 7, 14, 20, 27, 154
Workshop 30, 39, 42, 63, 70, 82, 91, 93,
    97, 101, 118, 129, 152